Susan Schramm peels back the onion . . . and breaks it down so anyone can make a Big Idea happen. Follow her system and your Big Idea just might become "The Next Big Thing."

—Andy Cunningham, Silicon Valley Brand Positioning Expert; Founder and CEO, The Cunningham Collective; Author, Get to Aha! Discover Your Positioning DNA and Dominate Your Competition

I've seen business and nonprofit leaders struggle to turn their vision into reality. Susan Schramm's book helps leaders develop an effective strategy to get an idea off the ground. But it also guides them to prepare for the risks and potential hurdles they'll face during implementation . . . invaluable advice for bringing your idea to life.

—Jeff Grubb, Investment Banker, Management Consultant, Philanthropist, and Trustee, MJ Murdock Charitable Trust

It's one thing to come up with a world-changing idea— and quite another to execute it. Whether you're in a large corporation or a startup, this book contains a wealth of real-world wisdom for making your dream happen . . . an ideal how-to manual for everyone who's dared to imagine a better way of doing things.

—Leslie Shannon, Head of Trend and Innovation Scouting, Nokia; Author, *Interconnected Realities: How the Metaverse Will Transform Our Relationship with Technology Forever*

Susan Schramm excels at distilling complex concepts into clear strategies. A rare combination of analytical precision and inspirational leadership . . . This is a must-read for leaders looking to transform bold ideas into reality.

—Harald Braun, Board Member, Investor, Executive Chairman, and CEO of Guident Corporation, Guiding Autonomous Vehicles to Safer Horizons

Everyone has ideas—but everyone has also seen terrific ideas that went nowhere. If you want to avoid that trap and really make things happen, this book will be a lively

and powerful guide. An interactive how-to manual for turning creative ideas into meaningful results in today's unpredictable environment.

—Alan Iny, Partner and Director, Global Lead for Creativity and Scenarios, Boston Consulting Group; Co-Author, *Thinking in New Boxes: A New Paradigm for Business Creativity*

*I've seen firsthand that risk, when properly understood and managed, becomes a catalyst. **Susan Schramm provides clear, practical steps to de-risk initiatives and turn big ideas into achievable goals. This book is a game-changer, not only for leaders but for the entire organization.***

—Brian Fontes, Chief Executive Officer, NENA, The 911 Association

***Too often, people shy away from openly discussing risk. Susan Schramm offers practical ways to de-risk your strategy that are easily understood regardless of your organization's size, background, or culture.** Don't miss this.*

—Patrice Tsague, Entrepreneur, Business Coach, and Chief Servant Officer, Nehemiah Entrepreneurship Community

***In a world that can feel increasingly risky, Susan Schramm delivers a world-class book on how to think differently and talk about risk as a positive force in strategy.** This must-have resource balances principles and practices to help you turn your vision into reality and impact.*

—Jay Allyson, Entrepreneur, Business Strategist, and Author, *Leveraged Consulting in the Digital Age and The AI Business Accelerator*

Effective problem-solving in business partnerships is about navigating differing viewpoints. Leaders will gain an edge by using Susan Schramm's "de-risk" system.

—Richard J. Chandler, MA, LPC, Executive Coach for Business Owners and Partners, "The Business Partners Counselor"

***Susan's years of hands-on experience shine through in this book. She's a proven change agent and strategic thinker, leading teams to re-engineer the way they work.** This has resulted in shorter product development cycle times,* *reduced inventory levels, innovative solutions for market launch, and ultimately operational results.*

—Karl Geng, Former CEO for Fortune 500 Tech Companies; Trustee, Civil Air Patrol Foundation

Susan Schramm delivers a practical framework for leaders ready to drive bold initiatives . . . Addressing risk directly and helping leaders communicate their vision in a way that resonates and mobilizes teams. *Invaluable.*

—Ben Decker, Business Communications Expert, Co-CEO, Decker Communications; Co-Author, *Communicate to Influence: How to Inspire Your Audience to Action*

A riveting read! Susan Schramm delivers valuable tools to drive success at every level. *An essential resource for achieving results in a dynamic environment.*

—Deepti Arora, Strategic Advisor, Former Chief Quality Officer, Nokia; Chair Emeritus, Telecommunications Industry Association

Through a blend of real-world examples and easy-to-follow frameworks, **this book offers actionable insights to effectively execute new strategies—whether you are an enthusiastic new startup, a global organization striving to shift gears, or new partners tackling a common vision.**

—Peggy Klingel, Growth Strategist, Head of Business Development Assured Allies; Former Director of Corporate Development, Allstate

With the number of nonprofits in North America growing every year, Susan Schramm's book arrives at a perfect time. *Many boards find themselves unprepared to navigate the complexities of governance, risk, and strategic planning. For nonprofit leaders looking to clarify their strategy, engage their boards more effectively, and steer their organizations toward lasting impact, this book will be a vital resource.*

—Christina Becker, Strategic Consultant and Founder, Canadian Nonprofit Academy

Susan Schramm strikes an excellent balance between sharing a point of view and a manifesto . . . **she gives hope to business leaders who are hesitant to admit they are stuck.** *A worthy read.*

—Howard Fields, Strategic Growth and Business Transformation
Expert, Fortune 500 Tech Executive

This book provides more than conceptual advice . . . it delivers a clear framework you can follow, along with practical tools you can apply immediately . . . a perfect companion for business, nonprofit, and church leaders who are striving to move forward faster.

—Jonathan Ankney, Founder and CEO, Small Business CFO;
Author, *Freedom to Serve*

What really sets this book apart is its deep understanding of purpose-driven leadership. It doesn't just help you clarify your strategy—it inspires you to align your vision with values, engage people with authenticity, and create a ripple effect of positive change.

—Danny Iny, Educator, Author, Founder and CEO, Mirasee

Even if your idea is a small seed of something that can be bigger—this book is useful.

—Tom Ruch, Fortune 500 Tech Executive;
Founder, School Ministry757

A master class packed with practical tools readers can use immediately. Susan Schramm's contagious passion . . . makes the process feel like a joy ride.

—Chantal Boeckman, Strategic Communication and Public Relations
Leader, Head of Global Digital Marketing, Amadeus IT Group

This isn't just another business book—it's a powerful call to leaders to build on a foundation of shared purpose.

—Pam Wolf, Entrepreneur; Co-Author, *Identity and Destiny: 7 Steps to a Purpose-Filled Life*

Susan Schramm helps you think through the risks and opportunities of your strategy and build a plan to inspire diverse people and organizations to help you achieve it. If you are committed to achieving big results while staying true to your faith and principles, you need to get, read, and implement this book.

—Ana Maria Lowry, Supply Chain Diversity Expert, Author,
President and CEO, A&P International

FAST TRACK
YOUR
BIG IDEA!

Navigate Risk, Move People to Action,
and Avoid Your Strategy Going Off Course

SUSAN BAILEY SCHRAMM

IMPACT PRESS
AMPLIFYING PURPOSE. ACCELERATING IMPACT.

Published by Impact Press, Livingston, Texas
www.impactpress.net

Visit the author's website at www.susanschramm.com.

Internet addresses given in this book were accurate at the time it went to press.

Printed in the United States of America

Cover and interior design by Anna Magruder

Illustrations were either purchased or created for the author by Nissa Milberger and Februalin Paquera Briones, inspired based on referenced sources except in the case of Business Model Canvas, which was distributed under a Creative Commons license from Strategyzer AG. "You Are Here" graphic created using images courtesy of Vecteezy. com.

Library of Congress Control Number: 2025910155

Paperback ISBN: 979-8-9991083-0-2
Hardcover ISBN: 979-8-9991083-1-9
eBook ISBN: 979-8-9991083-2-6

To all those who dare to take a risk and turn a big idea into reality—this book is for you. Whether you are strengthening communities, saving lives, or simply making your corner of the world a better place, I wrote this book to equip and encourage you to seize this moment.

Download the
Fast Track Your Big Idea!
Bonus Resources
for FREE

BUILD A FLYWHEEL TO
MOVE YOUR STRATEGY FORWARD

You can create an ACCELERATION ADVANTAGE™ for your strategy. Download these free Fast Track bonus resources today.

You'll find exercises, templates, checklists, a glossary, and recommended readings, all designed to help you:
- **De-risk your strategy to avoid common mistakes**
- **Align people to reduce friction**
- **Communicate to move people to action**
- **Adapt quickly to seize windows of opportunity**

Access your **FREE** bonus materials at
bonus.fasttrackyourbigidea.com

CONTENTS

Why You Need This Book 1

Section 1 **Are You Ready?** 11

    Chapter 1 The Thrill of Getting into the Driver's Seat. . .12

    Chapter 2 Why Changing Direction Is So Darn Hard. . .17

    Key Takeaways 22

Section 2 **Creating Your ACCELERATION ADVANTAGE™ 24**

    Chapter 3 Creating Momentum 25

    Chapter 4 Refining Your Strategy 28

    Chapter 5 It's All About *Them* 33

    Chapter 6 The Power of Transition 37

    Key Takeaways 42

Section 3 **Get in Gear: De-Risking Your Strategy for
Impact** **44**

    Chapter 7 Your Relationship with Risk 46

    Chapter 8 When NOT Talking about Risk Is Risky 52

    Chapter 9 The Power and the Trap of Assumptions . . 56

    Chapter 10 What Is De-Risking and Why Does It
    Matter? 59

    Chapter 11 Your ACCELERATION ADVANTAGE™:
    The De-Risk System for Impact® 61

    Key Takeaways 101

Section 4 **Overdrive: Aligning for Maximum Traction . .103**

    Chapter 12 Get on Board or on One Page? 105

    Chapter 13 Your ACCELERATION ADVANTAGE™:
    A Game Plan for Alignment. 107

    Chapter 14 The Most Important Alignment: Your Own .127

    Key Takeaways 132

Section 5 **Turbocharge: Communicating to Inspire Action** **134**

    Chapter 15 Today's Communication Conundrum 135

    Chapter 16 Communicating to Move People to Action 138

    Chapter 17 The Power of Consistency. 143

    Chapter 18 Your ACCELERATION ADVANTAGE™:
    A Strategic Message Playbook. 146

    Chapter 19 Putting a Strategic Message Playbook
    into Action 150

    Key Takeaways. 154

Section 6 **Shifting Gears: Adapting to Propel Results . .156**

    Chapter 20 An Uncertain Road Will Get Bumpy. 157

    Chapter 21 Your ACCELERATION ADVANTAGE™:
    An Adaptive Roadmap. 161

    Chapter 22 Becoming an Adaptive Leader 180

    Key Takeaways. 183

Conclusion: Fast Track Your Strategy Today. 185

Resources to Support You on Your Journey 187

Glossary. 190

Notes 191

In Appreciation. 196

About the Author. 197

Why You Need This Book

Vision without action is merely a dream.
Action without vision just passes the time.
Vision with action can change the world.
Joel Barker, futurist, filmmaker, and author

Never doubt a small group of thoughtful, committed citizens
can change the world; indeed, it's the only thing that ever has.
Margaret Mead, cultural anthropologist, teacher, and author

From Idea to Impact

Do you have a big idea that could change the world?

You may be on a personal mission to tackle a big problem. Or you may be part of an organization with a big vision. You may lead a high-stakes initiative with the potential to transform your organization, develop a new product, create a new program, or implement a new way of working.

Or do you have a small idea with big potential?

Even if changing the world is not your goal, you have an idea for improving your corner of the world. Big ideas start with small inspiration. You may not have it all figured out yet, but your idea has the potential to be successful, profitable, and satisfying.

Whether it's a game-changing vision or a small change that has big possibilities—you have the potential to improve lives, transform industries, and create lasting value. But moving from vision to execution isn't easy. It requires more than inspiration.

Are you engaging the right people to help you turn your idea into reality?

You can't achieve your big idea alone. The success of a new strategy depends on bringing the right people along with you: peers, employees, experts, funders, partners, customers, suppliers, volunteers, community leaders, advisors, advocates, and even critics who can challenge your thinking and sharpen your strategy.

The success of your strategy will depend on inspiring people to take action.

No matter how clear your vision or how brilliant your strategy, your success will depend on inspiring people to take action.

Reality Check: Your Journey Will Get Bumpy

I'm going to be blunt: *there's a very real risk that your strategy won't go as planned.* In fact, I guarantee it.

Every time you take a new direction, there are risks: the risk of getting lost, traffic jams, and delays, the risk that a pothole blows out your tire, or the risk you miss a turn. But despite these risks, people take new roads to new places every day. To fast track your big idea, you need to plan for the risk as well.

Leading a new strategy can be exciting and energizing, but it can also be frustrating, exhausting, and a bit daunting. Getting everyone on the same page takes work, from your leadership team to your board of directors and funders, from your employees and volunteers to your partners and customers. It means dealing with unending questions and sometimes even questioning yourself.

I understand. And I can help you get through it.

Though my roles and titles have changed over the years, my focus has always been the same: to launch big ideas (or get them back on track!) so that other people will join in. I've launched new products and services, new programs and brands, new partnerships, joint ventures, and new companies.

And while there were many successes, *sometimes it got pretty bumpy!*

I remember the sweaty palms and sleepless nights over "make or break" launches. As I tried to confidently persuade everyone we were on the right track, I often worried, "Why aren't we moving faster? How can I make sure we get results? *What if we fail?*"

These questions were often the most challenging when working with purpose-led organizations—businesses striving to achieve community, social, or environmental impact; associations and alliances focused on improving how the industry delivers value; and charities and faith-based groups addressing urgent real-world problems.

I've met many inspiring and committed leaders within these organizations. Yet many become so focused on the mission that they underestimate what it takes to get their big idea off the ground. In their zeal to achieve results, leaders—especially purpose-driven leaders—often skip the fundamentals that would ensure their strategy will stick.

When the fundamentals are skipped, worthy initiatives get derailed, commitments are missed, people get frustrated, and mission impact is delayed. Even worse, the credibility of the entire organization can be hurt, funding can dry up, and good people can end up abandoning ship.

From Sleepless Nights to a Call to Action

Frustrated by seeing so many great ideas get stuck or never become reality, I went back and took a hard look at launches I'd been involved with that hadn't gone well. I did research and interviewed leaders who were willing to share their triumphs and their scars.

It is the human element *that will determine the success or failure of a strategy.*

Across all these experiences, a theme emerged: *It is the human element that will determine the success or failure of a strategy.*

Yet these risks are often underestimated or ignored entirely. New strategies consistently fail when leaders underestimate the role people play in translating a big vision into reality.

How This Book Can Help

The truth is that the success or failure of your strategy hinges on one critical factor: the people who need to take action. You can have the most brilliant plan, but if you overlook the human element—their needs, concerns, and motivations—it will fail.

The good news? The keys to success aren't magic. They're straightforward and within your reach—but ignore them at your peril.

I wrote this book to distill those keys into practical steps, helping you inspire people to take action and achieve results faster. All you need is a solid strategy and someone to walk with you on the journey. This book will help you clarify your strategy, navigate risks, and guide you from start to finish as you turn your big idea into reality.

Who Is This Book For?

This book is a practical guide for leaders driving a new strategy to achieve results faster. It will help you navigate the risks and inspire people to take action. You can use this book in every one of the following situations:

Are you taking your organization in a new direction?

> If you are leading people to drive a new strategy, use this book to identify the risks and build a game plan to enlist people to *shift with you*—and avoid having your strategy get stuck down the road.

Are you exploring a big idea?

> You may be in the discovery stage, still investigating the problem you want to solve. Use this book as a step-by-step roadmap to clarify your ideas up front and get a faster start.

Have you already launched—but you're stalled?

If a new initiative isn't going as planned, you and your team may be struggling with where to go next. Use this book as an opportunity to take a big breath, recharge, and move forward more confidently.

Are you an "intrapreneur" driving a new initiative?

The great news is your organization has lots of people and resources—but they don't all work for you! Use this book to help you navigate the risks and more confidently enlist people across many functions to do something new.

Do you lead a nonprofit?

You may have a new strategy to achieve a noble mission but are concerned it will get stalled. Use this book to identify key resources and launch processes, clarify the risks up front, and gain the confidence and support of funders and volunteers whose help you need.

Are you making a big transition?

You may be taking a giant leap from the familiar to the unfamiliar. Whether you are launching your own business after years as an employee or expanding into a new country, use this book to help you plan for the risks of the unfamiliar.

Have you been tapped by others to lead a high-stakes strategy?

Your big idea was someone else's brainchild, but you've been asked to bring it to life. Use this book to clarify your strategy, call out the risks, and align the right people to help. (If the person who tapped you for this role gave you this book, congratulations! You already have someone in your court!)

Are you an advisor, a board member, an investor, or a donor?

You advise leaders because they value your experience, expertise, and insights. Unfortunately, they don't always apply them! Use this book to prompt meaningful dialogue with those you guide who are struggling to drive a new strategy.

Is your big idea a calling?

> You may be stepping out in faith to pursue your big idea. My faith in God fuels me to take risks for a greater purpose. Even if you aren't very spiritual, this book is guaranteed to provide great value. But if you are, this book provides an opportunity to consider how your faith and values shape your strategy as you lead with integrity.

Did you see a theme in all of these different roles and situations? What these leaders have in common is that they are:

- Committed to making a big idea a reality
- Urgent about making progress faster
- Willing to do the work to bring others along with them
- Courageous and humble enough to deal with the risks and try a new approach.

So if *you* have a big idea and are eager to see more progress, this book is for you, no matter your role or the stage or size of your organization.

This Book Will Not Work for You If . . .

If your big idea does *not* require people to get involved, then this book is *not* designed for you. If you can do all the work yourself or if you believe technology will achieve your mission without getting people to work together in new ways, then you do *not* need the concepts we will explore in this book.

To be clear, in today's world, you *must* leverage technology, or you will be at a competitive disadvantage. But whether your strategy involves artificial intelligence or autonomous systems, augmented or virtual reality, robotics or quantum computing, technology on autopilot can fumble when faced with surprises—especially when your strategy requires people to do something new. Even the most critical tech-enabled solutions require a dash of human collaboration, sometimes to nudge technology back on track when it gets stuck!

So if you *know* you need *people* to help you achieve an idea to improve the world around you, you're in the right place.

Is Faster Better?

A frequent concern I hear from leadership teams and boards is that they aren't moving fast enough:

> "We're not making enough headway."

> "We're spinning our wheels."

> "I had hoped we could have accomplished more by now."

> "We're getting stuck."

Do you ever feel this way?

When you've invested a great deal of time, energy, and resources, it's understandable that you want to see results quickly. You may have made a significant commitment to others. There may be severe financial consequences. Your pride and reputation may be on the line. You might be on a mission to solve an important problem in the world and concerned that every delay means this serious problem persists.

When you need people to help you accomplish your big idea, you may need to slow down to go faster.

This book is jam-packed with ways to sidestep common mistakes, avoid wasted effort, and streamline what you can do to speed results. But heads up! Sometimes, you will need to *slow down to go faster*.

When you need *people* to help you accomplish your big idea, it is going to require extra work. This book will help you clarify your big idea and ensure people understand what you are trying to achieve. It provides specific ways to anticipate what they will need so that they are ready and able to take action. You will learn how to deal with risks and adapt together when you encounter surprises.

All of this will take a little more time and effort up front. But I guarantee that this work has a payoff. It will help you avoid delays, confusion, and false starts. It will help you enlist the people and resources you need to get things done faster and avoid having people abandon ship when you run into bumps in the road. Though it will take time, bringing people along with you on your journey will have the greatest rewards.

How This Book Is Organized

This book is a practical guide to help you execute a new strategy to achieve a big idea. It provides specific actions you can apply today.

In Section 1, you will explore your readiness for this journey and what got you to this point. In Section 2, you will learn about how to create momentum with an ACCELERATION ADVANTAGE™ and three strategic concepts that provide important context: the Strategy Process, Market Adoption, and the Transition Mindset.

In Sections 3 through 6, we dive into the four ways you can create an ACCELERATION ADVANTAGE™ by:

- Proactively addressing the risks of your strategy
- Aligning people to implement your strategy together
- Communicating your strategy so people understand and take action
- Adapting to surprises, disruptions, and opportunities.

Throughout the book, I'll point out specific actions you can take to avoid common mistakes. We'll also discuss the mindset you and your team will need to apply to remain resilient, whatever comes your way.

I've provided exercises, templates, and checklists to use with your team. Each section has a list of Key Takeaways and a "Notes and Action Steps" area to jot down the nuggets you've learned and how you intend to apply them.

Visit bonus.fasttrackyourbigidea.com for more resouces to support you. There are tools and checklists you can download, a glossary to help with unfamiliar terminology, and a reading list to help you dive deeper.

How to Read This Book

I encourage you to make this book your own. View it as a canvas for your thoughts: jot notes in the margins, fold down pages to go back to, underline examples that resonate, and list names of people you want to talk to about a topic. I hope you'll share this book with others. But when you do, give them a fresh copy. This one will be full of *your* thoughts! (If you are reading or listening to an electronic version of the book, set aside a blank notebook to jot down your ideas and "ah-ha's" in one place!)

One caution: This book is chock-full of ideas and how-to's for each stage of a strategy. Do not get overwhelmed! *Not every point applies to your journey right now.* Identify the points that resonate most and the ones you can implement quickly. If you see concepts that you would like to come back to, highlight them to review down the road.

Here's how to read this book to get the most value:

1. *If a topic is new to you or one that you struggle with*, dive in deep! Note the concepts that are most relevant to your situation. Jot down your own examples. After reading the section, go back and do the exercises. When you get to "Notes and Action Steps," identify two or three actions you commit to implementing *right now*.

2. *If you are familiar with a topic*, scan with an eye for new angles (I promise they're there!) and make sure you understand the Key Takeaways. Jot down any new insights and flag any actions you can implement. (Just because an idea is familiar doesn't mean you should skip it!)

3. *Once you've completed the book*, step back and review your "Notes and Action Steps" from each sec-

tion and create your own roadmap to apply them. Use this book as a resource as you reach each new stage in your strategy. It can also be a source of new ideas when you get stuck or need some inspiration down the road.

A Compass for Your Journey

By the time you finish this book, you will:

- Understand the challenges and common mistakes leaders make when striving to achieve a big idea.

- Be clear about the fundamentals when defining and implementing a new strategy and getting people to join you.

- Be ready to deal with the risks and potholes down the road as you implement your strategy.

- Feel more confident leading others in a new direction despite the uncertainty.

Wherever you are on your journey, I look forward to offering roadside support to help you merge into the fast lane. So buckle up: we're going to have fun!

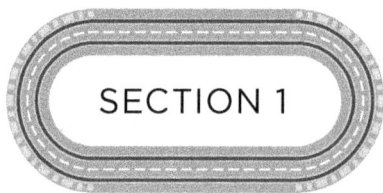

SECTION 1

ARE YOU READY?

The miracle isn't that I finished.
The miracle is that I had the courage to start.
John Bingham, marathon runner and author

A challenging journey requires courage, whether you're crossing a desert, navigating treacherous mountains, traversing a dense forest, or tackling a grueling racecourse. But when you have taken time to get ready and are physically and mentally prepared for what's ahead, you can more confidently face whatever obstacles come your way. The challenges may be daunting, but your preparation will help you overcome them step by step.

Driving a new strategy requires courage too. Leading others in a new direction is an exhilarating, frustrating, and humbling opportunity. Being prepared will help you overcome the challenges.

What has led you to this point? Are you ready?

In this first section, we will explore how you are uniquely positioned to lead others at this moment in time and what you'll need to consider as you prepare to achieve your big idea.

CHAPTER 1

THE THRILL OF GETTING INTO THE DRIVER'S SEAT

Getting my driver's permit and driving for the first time was a game changer.

That afternoon, I got into the driver's seat, buckled my seat belt, checked the mirrors, turned the key, pressed the gas pedal—and *lurched* forward with such a jolt that my mom yelled out loud and my sister jumped out of the car!

Though I had studied the rules of the road and thought I knew what to do, being in the driver's seat felt entirely different. I had to consider more as a driver than I'd ever noticed as a passenger. I had to be gentle on the gas and carefully evaluate the traffic before I eased onto the road. I gained a new respect for this giant, heavy machine I was now in charge of.

In much the same way, you are now in the driver's seat for your big idea. You may have spun your wheels a bit at the start. You may need to clarify the scope of what you are responsible for, understand the environment, correctly read the feedback you're getting, and try new approaches when something doesn't work—but you are on your way.

Let's start by considering what got you to this point. *Why* are you in the driver's seat for your strategy? Are you excited by the possibilities? Is it urgent that you act now? Did someone else task you with this leadership?

Excitement: When You Can See What's Possible

Sometimes I've believed as many as six impossible things before breakfast.

Lewis Carroll, mathematician, poet, and author of *Alice's Adventures in Wonderland*

Your big idea may have hit you suddenly as a "Eureka!" moment, or it may have been an inkling that grew over time. You may have initially thought, "That's crazy!" but over time, it grew on you, and you started to think, "Heck, maybe this could work!" The excitement of possibilities gives you energy.

I see this excitement every day with leaders driving a new direction. We'll be in the middle of a messy discussion about how things may be stuck or not working fast enough. Frustration is high, and there's a negative cloud in the room.

But then the conversation will go back to their WHY, their big idea. Everyone's eyes light up, they start talking faster, and the energy comes back into the room like a refreshing breeze. People excitedly talk about the critical problem they are working to solve and their vision for how the world will be better. They talk about the impact this change can have on their customers and beneficiaries, their employees and volunteers, and their community. They talk about how satisfied and proud they will feel when they have achieved the impact they aspire to. The room becomes electric.

Being excited about your destination is critical. It helps you overcome complex challenges along the way and inspires others.

But what if you've been asked to step in and solve a problem you're ambivalent about? The truth is you will be at a disadvantage as a leader. People see through fake interest and obligatory rah-rah. People who need to take action will remain skeptical and drag their feet. Over time, you may feel skeptical and worn out too.

How can you stir up some genuine enthusiasm to solve the problem if you currently don't feel it? By digging a little deeper:

- *Walk in the shoes of real people* experiencing the problem. Talk to people living with the consequences and understand the impact they're feeling.

- *Dream with others.* Talk to people about what life could be like once the problem is solved. What happens when daily irritations go away? What will they do with the time they get back? Whose lives could be impacted?

- *Explore how you can personally grow* from this effort. Can you gain a new skill, experience, or responsibility by leading this strategy? Can you design the project to make this more likely?

- *Break it down and celebrate each step.* How could you celebrate progress at each milestone? What kind of celebration or reward will most motivate you and your team?

- *Tap someone else's energy.* Find a leader who is genuinely energized about the problem and invite that person to lead with you. Supporting and collaborating together can be rewarding, and their energy and attitude can be infectious.

When the excitement of possibilities fuels you, leading others can be a true adventure. On the flip side, fear of the consequences of *not* taking action can also be a source of motivation!

Urgency: When *Not* Changing Direction Means Falling Behind

Satya Nadella realized he had a problem. He had just been announced as the CEO of Microsoft, and the company was struggling.

Microsoft had dominated the desktop software market for decades, but mobile devices and cloud computing were reshaping the industry. Their once-dominant operating system, Windows, was fighting challenges from mobile platforms like iOS and Android. Traditional software licensing fees, which had been their bread and butter for years, were trailing off. The company faced increasing competition from new cloud-based providers, like Amazon Web Services and Google Cloud.

Nadella realized the seriousness of the situation. *Doing things the same old way was simply not going to be acceptable.*

So Nadella decided to pivot the company and become laser focused on cloud-based offerings and artificial intelligence. It was a difficult change for an organization as large as Microsoft, but that one decision set the stage for the company's dramatic turnaround as it catapulted to become a leader in the cloud computing and AI markets.

Nadella's story is one of a strong leader who recognized that the environment had fundamentally changed and decided to courageously take a new direction.

A gradual shift in the market can result in a need to pivot. But a sudden shock can drive the need for a shift much faster. The COVID-19 pandemic forced leaders of companies large and small to quickly change their strategy. The old way was suddenly not going to work, and even reluctant leaders changed direction overnight:

- Restaurant owners shifted to contactless digital payments, expanding services through delivery, takeout, and online platforms.

- Doctors adopted virtual triage and wearable monitoring to assess symptoms, prioritize care, and manage chronic conditions—all without in-person visits.

- Pastors who were not able to meet in person shifted church services online, even convening virtual choirs.

The urgency was real, and standing still was not an option.

Whether you see a sudden change in market demand, costs, or available resources or you have a slow realization that the way you're doing things isn't working anymore, *don't ignore it*. When the old way is no longer acceptable, a strong leader must decide to act and courageously take a new direction.

Stepping Up: When Others Need You to Drive

Sometimes people end up in the driver's seat *because others need them to lead:*

- In the Biblical story of Exodus, God called Moses to lead the Israelites out of Egypt. Moses objected because he felt he was too old and "slow of speech and of tongue," but God believed otherwise.[1]

- Though she was only seventeen years old and a peasant girl, Joan of Arc's devotion to France convinced Charles VII that he needed Joan's help to save France from English domination.

- Though unsuccessful in business and a known drinker, Ulysses Grant was President Lincoln's choice to lead the Union army at a crucial time in the American Civil War. Lincoln said about Grant, "He makes things git! Where he is, things move!"[2]

That's right. Some of the most significant change agents in history, like Moses, Joan of Arc, and Ulysses Grant, stepped up when *others* saw their potential.

You may not have sought your place in the driver's seat, but you are leading right now because others believe you have what it takes. This can be flattering, daunting, or both. The great news is that others have confidence in you as you step up.

You're Here for a Reason

Whatever brought you to this moment, you are in the driver's seat to lead a new strategy for a reason. Whether it's due to a sudden change or a gradual realization that you need to change direction, you have the potential to make an impact. How you lead others will be critical. Be intentional, as the road ahead will not always be easy.

CHAPTER 2

WHY CHANGING DIRECTION IS SO DARN HARD

The CEO sitting across from me looked dejected. He had been tapped from the start-up world to help a large company innovate faster. The reports stacked in front of him showed that his new strategy was not panning out. Pressure from the board and investors was high.

> "We could have jumped ahead of the market like a speed boat. Turns out we're just a big clunky tanker!" he lamented.

The *easy* thing to do was to abandon the strategy. The *hard* thing to do was to turn things around. We needed to help him find the steering wheel.

I find leaders in organizations of all sizes are often surprised when their strategy doesn't pan out. They shouldn't be. Failure is often a necessary part of making a change. What matters most is what you do next.

The Difficult Truth: Most New Strategies Fail

If you are going to invest the time and energy to lead a new strategy, it's important to start with your eyes wide open. Let's look at a few statistics:

- 48% of new businesses fail within the first five years; 65% fail within ten years.[3]

- 80% of early-stage venture capital investments never meet their financial targets.[4]

- 70% of change programs initiated by established companies fail.[5]

- From 60% to 95% of digital transformation initiatives do not achieve the original objectives.[6]

- Approximately 30% of nonprofits fail to exist after ten years.[7]

Pretty sobering, isn't it? The consequences can vary. Sometimes failure means an entire organization suddenly no longer exists or that the CEO or senior leaders are replaced. Sometimes it means an expected improvement doesn't pan out, and the organization has to figure out how to shift gears yet again. In all cases, a lot of people put their time and effort into a direction that didn't work out as planned, and the disappointment is real.

There are many reasons why new strategies don't work out. After the fact, analysts will point to factors like missed market windows, poor capitalization, or poor execution. But I have found through my experience and research that there are three things too many leaders *underestimate* when taking an established organization in a new direction:

1. *Your new strategy requires that you take a lot of people with you.*

    Why this matters: If your strategy requires people to take new action, they need to be prepared or your strategy will falter.

    My frustrated CEO friend was right. He launched the new strategy like he was driving a speedboat—by himself! But executing his big idea in an established company meant he had to get a LOT more people in the boat with him.

    Sure, a speedboat can turn quickly on a whim, but big, clunky tankers can successfully change direction too. They do it every day. To make it happen, the ship's captain enlists all those people who must do something differently. Not just the officers on the bridge, but those in the engine room, those who plan fuel and supplies, and even the cook, who needs to know about the changing course so they can support those on the front line.

Engaging all functions and roles when you make a change in direction is critical to success, whether you are leading a large organization or small team.

2. *Your new strategy requires massive reserves of energy to execute.*

   Why this matters: If people in your organization do not have the *capacity* to focus on your new strategy, it will falter.

   When the Canadian icebreaker tanker ship *Louis S. St. Laurent* speeds through open water, it burns 7,925 gallons of fuel a day. But when it runs into thick ice and needs to take a turn, it has to use all five of its engines and burns 24,000 gallons of fuel, or 300% more per day!

   Your team might have the same challenge. When you're executing a familiar process, you can deliver very high quality at volume. People know what to do, and productivity is high. But when you shift gears and people run into unexpected roadblocks, you can burn up a lot of energy, which turns into missed deadlines, mistakes, and complaints.

   Sometimes it's simply a matter of too many priorities. The top three priorities handed down from the CEO translate into ten priorities from the first-line manager, which turn into thirty priorities for front-line employees. But there is a limit to how much energy a person can invest in each priority.

   Making sure your organization has the *capacity to execute a new strategy,* whether that means mental capacity or time, is critical if you're going to succeed.

3. *Your new strategy is just a guess.*

Why this matters: Defining your assumptions and testing them as early as possible can help you navigate the risks of your new strategy.

Just getting clear on the assumptions you're making and prioritizing them in terms of their impact is an essential first step. Determining early which assumptions are false allows you to rethink your plan before investing so much of your time, talent, or treasure that you simply cannot recover.

If you prepare to execute your strategy by looping in all the people who need to be involved, ensuring you have enough time and energy to devote to its success and double-checking your assumptions, you'll have a significant head start on avoiding many common pitfalls. This will also help you deal with the inevitable uncertainty to come.

Coping with the Uncertainty Factor

You are leading your new strategy in an uncertain world.

The International Monetary Fund produces the World Uncertainty Index. It measures the number of times the word "uncertainty" is used when countries report what is going on in their economy and political landscape. Through terrorism, financial crises, and global shifts in power, the World Uncertainty Index has continued to rise over time. Not surprisingly, during the worldwide pandemic and supply chain disruptions, the index spiked to its highest in over thirty years.[8]

But uncertainty is not new! Feelings of uncertainty are as old as human history. Imagine if the World Uncertainty Index had tracked what people were saying during the Black Death plague in the 1300s or in the 1900s during two World Wars. Don't you think we would have seen a few spikes back then too?

What makes today's uncertainty feel worse than it did in the past? *We can't escape it.* Our tightly interconnected world makes us more *aware* of change. While this rapid dissemination of information enables us to stay informed and make better choices, it also amplifies the uncertainty we experience. This constant stream of new information, both positive and negative, can create an environment where every change feels like it could have immediate implications and even create imminent danger. As a result, our day-to-day world feels more unpredictable and unsettling than it did for previous generations.

Why does this matter? When people receive a constant stream of uncertainty, it can be paralyzing! *When uncertainty gets too high, even leaders can freeze.* The weight of potential consequences makes it tempting to maintain the status quo.

McKinsey Consulting has done research on the relationship between companies' organizational health and their financial performance. The research showed that "unhealthy" organizations—those without sufficient organizational skills to respond to change—were more than twice as likely to go bankrupt as their "healthy" counterparts.[9]

When you plan for how to weather the storm, early failures can become stepping stones.

In times of overwhelming uncertainty, teams can get stuck because their leaders get stuck. But when you plan for how to weather the storm, early failures can become stepping stones. You foster a culture of adaptability, developing the capabilities to anticipate and adapt to uncertainty, seize opportunities, and create a competitive advantage.

Ready to Drive

For whatever reason, you are now in the driver's seat to achieve a big idea. When you prepare your strategy with your eyes wide open, knowing that there will be uncertainty and roadblocks along the way, you're more likely to achieve your vision. Let's start by figuring out where you are on your journey.

Section 1 Key Takeaways
Are You Ready?

To achieve your big idea, it is essential to prepare for the journey ahead:

- *Be intentional.* You are in the driver's seat to lead a new strategy for a reason. Whatever brought you to this moment, how you lead others will be critical.

- *Many new strategies fail.* Going in humbly, with your eyes wide open, can help you recognize early warning signs and be ready to adapt.

- *You have to take a lot of people with you.* You will need to engage a lot more people than you expected for your strategy to succeed, and many of them don't work for you. It's worth the effort, but it will take work.

- *A new strategy requires a lot of energy.* Ensure your team has the physical and mental capacity to execute, or you may run out of gas.

- *Your new strategy is just a guess.* Get very clear about the assumptions you are making and be prepared to change your plans if your assumptions prove incorrect.

- *You can create a competitive advantage* by managing uncertainty intentionally and being able to quickly adapt when your environment changes.

Section 1 Notes and Action Steps
Are You Ready?

(Jot down two to three things that jumped out that you can quickly apply.)

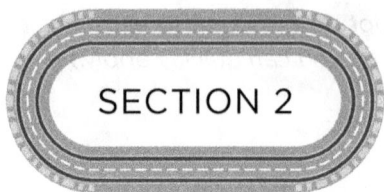

SECTION 2

CREATING YOUR
ACCELERATION ADVANTAGE™

To achieve great things, two things are needed:
A plan, and not quite enough time.
Leonard Bernstein, composer, conductor, and educator

When it comes to winning a high-speed car race, is it the car, the driver, or the team that's most important? This question has sparked debates for years. The sight of the winning driver stepping out at the finish line excites fans, yet most races are decided before the drivers even hit the track. The secret to winning lies in combining the strengths of the car, driver, and support team. Successful teams stay on top by effectively doing this.

Much like racing teams, people who champion a new idea or project are impatient to begin. I created the ACCELERATION ADVANTAGE™ to provide a cohesive approach. It will help you not only get a solid start but continue to build momentum and sustain your strategy over time.

CHAPTER 3

CREATING MOMENTUM

Have you heard of the flywheel effect? It's a powerful concept for understanding the multifaceted nature of driving a successful strategy.

For those unfamiliar, a flywheel is a circular disc used in various engines, from steam engines to race cars. It helps get the machine moving and stores energy that keeps it going once it is started. Each rotation builds momentum, enabling the engine to run faster and more efficiently.

When applied to the marketplace, the flywheel effect means that small wins accumulate over time, creating momentum and sustaining growth through continuous, incremental improvements.

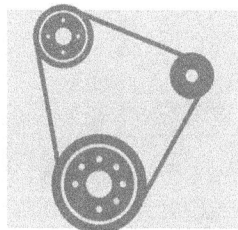

A Flywheel Creates Momentum

I've found that the best way to leverage the flywheel concept for a new strategy is to consistently apply four essential factors:

- *De-risking your strategy* to avoid common mistakes

- *Aligning people* to reduce friction

- *Communicating* to move people to action and speed results

- *Adapting quickly* to seize windows of opportunity.

Applying even *one* of these four success factors will move your strategy forward. But together, they reinforce each other and help create your own ACCELERATION ADVANTAGE™.

As you use them, these factors will become organic for you and your team, simply part of *how we do things here*. As you implement your strategy, you can lead more confidently, knowing that with every turn of your own flywheel, you are also building momentum.

Throughout this book, we'll dive into each of these ACCELERATION ADVANTAGE™ factors. You'll learn why they work, how to apply them, and how they build upon each other over time. You will learn ways to leverage them at different stages of your strategy and in different situations to get results faster.

But keep in mind: accelerating to go faster is only helpful when you know where you're going! Let's talk about what's ahead.

The ACCELERATION ADVANTAGE™
Go to Market Impact LLC

Where Are You Headed?

A few years ago, on a business trip to Tokyo, I decided to do a little sightseeing the day before a big meeting. Despite the fact that I spoke absolutely no Japanese (and had no translator app!), I chose to explore the city without a guide to get steeped in the culture.

As I stepped onto the street, I was confronted by a sea of faces, sounds, and language very different from my own. I explored the bustling Tokyo fish market, beautiful tea gardens, and temples.

As it got dark, I decided to head back to the hotel and prepare for the next day. I walked and walked. And I walked. Nothing looked familiar. After an hour, I finally had to admit it: *I was lost*.

My heart started to race. It was dark. I was by myself. I didn't know how to ask for directions. And if I were given directions, I wouldn't understand what they meant! I was getting a little panicky when I spied a kiosk next to a metro entrance. And there it was: A *map* with a *BIG RED ARROW*!

Though I didn't understand Japanese characters, I knew the big red arrow meant "You Are Here." And suddenly, I calmed down. I had actually been walking an entire hour in the wrong direction! But it was okay. I now knew where I was and where I was trying to go.

You Are Here

A "You Are Here" sign provides *context* as you make your way on a journey. When you have a map and a plan for where you are, you can get an idea of what's ahead and identify places you might want to explore along the way. And when you get stuck, knowing where you are can help you get oriented so you can calm down and get back on track.

In the next few chapters, we'll examine three strategic concepts that provide important context for you to keep your strategy on course and moving forward: the Strategy Process, Market Adoption, and the Transition Mindset. Understanding each concept will help you steer more confidently. The first concept concerns how to build a strategy that will stick.

CHAPTER 4

REFINING YOUR STRATEGY

A quick Google search for "how to build a strategy" will yield lots of good information and almost too many good ideas. It is easy to get lost in the possibilities and never get started. On the other hand, new strategies are often launched with great fanfare but fizzle out. People get confused and disillusioned. Work is wasted. Strategies stall.

Building a successful strategy isn't about putting a bunch of bold statements on PowerPoint slides and announcing with fireworks!

To execute a new strategy, a structured approach helps people navigate the risks, clarify priorities, and mobilize people to act. *Much like any journey, for your strategy to succeed, there are three elements you'll need to plan for:*

1. *Agree to a goal.* When taking a road trip, you need a specific physical destination that you can point to on a map. The more specific you are, the more easily you can plan your route to get there. To lead others to achieve your big idea, you will also need to be able to answer the question: "What are we trying to achieve?" That's your goal. Your strategy will be your game plan to achieve it.

2. *Allocate your resources thoughtfully.* A successful journey requires budgeting enough to cover gas, meals and snacks, lodging, and fun, with enough left

over to handle emergencies. In the same way, driving a new strategy requires a reasonable budget and being smart about using your resources—the time, talent, and treasure of your employees, volunteers, suppliers, partners, funders, and supporters.

3. *Define activities that create a unique result.* Our family's most memorable trips involve doing something different: exploring a new city, taking a new route, or quirky travel rituals like visiting the highest point of every state. Your strategy requires that you define unique ways to create value and differentiate your organization from others. These activities might include how you deliver services, how you ensure quality, or how you treat people in everyday interactions. Doing things the way everyone else does may help improve efficiencies, but identifying what you do uniquely will set you apart. It will also help you engage others to join you.

With these three elements of your strategy in place, people will be better equipped to take action and stay aligned, even when unexpected challenges arise.

To sustain your strategy, it is essential to understand and prepare for each stage of the Strategy Process, which I've described below. As you read through each stage and the

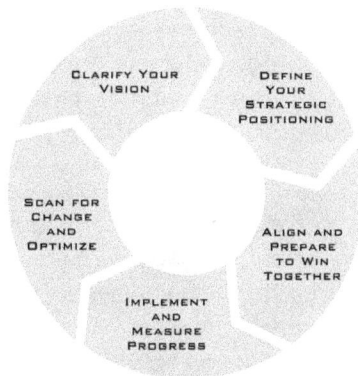

CLARIFY YOUR VISION

DEFINE YOUR STRATEGIC POSITIONING

SCAN FOR CHANGE AND OPTIMIZE

ALIGN AND PREPARE TO WIN TOGETHER

IMPLEMENT AND MEASURE PROGRESS

The Strategy Process
Go to Market Impact LLC

challenges to be prepared for, consider the following: Do any of these challenges seem familiar? Where are you now? What's next?

The Strategy Process

Stage 1: Clarify Your Vision

Many leaders confuse their *vision* with a fluffy "someday" tagline. Your vision can fuel your organization to accomplish great things—but only if you are clear about what "someday" looks like!

Avoid fluffy platitudes (e.g., "Building a brighter future!" or "Pioneering a path to unparalleled success!") and get specific about your vision: What is the real problem you want to solve? What will be different when you're successful? Who will care? Can your whole team describe the same vision? How can they each play a part? Ensure everyone is journeying to the same place by clarifying your vision as a team. (We'll go into this more in Section 3.)

Stage 2: Define Your Strategic Positioning

Your strategic positioning is the foundation for your strategy. It's where you intend to play and how you will win.

Sometimes leaders fall in love with their big idea and immediately jump in to start executing, expecting others to do the same. But if your strategy requires people to do something new and invest their time, talent, or treasure, they are likely to ask a few questions first: *Who are you? What do you stand for? What are you trying to achieve?*

Defining your strategic positioning helps others quickly understand why they should engage with you. Skip this stage, and decisions and results will be delayed. (The work you'll do in Section 3 lays the groundwork for your Strategic Positioning; in Section 5 we'll focus on how to best communicate it.)

Stage 3: Align and Prepare to Win Together

For some leaders, this stage can be the most frustrating! When *you* see the vision and how you want to get there, it's easy to get impatient with those who don't.

But even the best strategy will fail if people are confused, skeptical, or not aligned! Studies show that highly aligned organizations grow revenue 58% faster than those that are unaligned and unprepared.[10]

Even the best strategy will fail if people are confused, skeptical, or not aligned!

Aligning for a new strategy means bringing people together to support each other. Who has to take action to succeed? Are they prepared? Translate your vision into strategic goals, objectives, and milestones, and assign each one to a person or team with clear roles and responsibilities. Yes, it takes a little more time. But getting the alignment right will speed results by eliminating confusion. It will also help you avoid painful frustration along the way. ("Aligning for maximum traction" is the focus of Section 4.)

Stage 4: Implement and Measure Progress

This stage of the Strategy Process can be one of the most satisfying—and the most complex. The good news is that you can start seeing your vision's real-world impact! But this is also where you are confronted with the hard reality that some of your assumptions are wrong, and things don't work as expected. Here, you can also easily get lost in the details. Your team can get overwhelmed, disillusioned, and stuck.

In this stage, communicating to move people to action is critical. (Section 5 will provide practical ways to accomplish this.)

Stage 5: Scan for Change and Optimize

Even good leaders can become overly invested in their perfect plans and ignore signals that the environment has changed. This can kill a good strategy.

In this stage, you need to establish a regular cadence for sensing changing trends and evaluating your strategic options. Regularly thinking through "What If" scenarios can help your organization prepare for change.

The trick is to not only collect data but be willing to act on it! Regularly recalibrating as a team can help you adapt your business model, mitigate risk, and seize new opportunities.

The "last" stage of this Strategy Process is never finished. A healthy organization continues to adapt and create a sustainable competitive advantage as the journey continues. (You'll find ways to make a regular habit of "What If" Thinking in Sections 3 and 6.)

So where are *you* in your Strategy Process Journey? Whatever stage you are in, celebrate the progress you are making! Each stage is an important step in translating your big idea into reality, but it will require that people want to join you.

CHAPTER 5

IT'S ALL ABOUT *THEM*

When you're driving a high-stakes strategy, getting people to jump in and join you takes work. When they don't, it can be frustrating. The problem is that a new idea is perceived as risky. People evaluate your strategy and whether to join you based on how they view that risk.

You may call it discerning. Or you may call it stubborn. But it's human.

That's what Everett Rogers, the renowned originator of the term "early adopter," figured out. He grew up on a farm in western Iowa. As a student at Iowa State, he worked on new technology to improve corn yields by 20%. The potential to feed millions inspired him.

But Rogers got frustrated when he shared this powerful innovation with local farmers. His big idea fell on hard soil. Not even his dad was interested! Even after Rogers persuaded farmers to try his method in one field, it could take up to seven years for them to adopt it for their whole farm!

Everett Rogers was baffled. *What makes some people jump on innovation while others wait for years or lifetimes?*

He figured out that if you want 100% of the people to adopt a new idea or innovation, you need to address each group and understand their unique perspective.

His research found that all of us tend to fall into one of five groups when adopting new ideas:

INNOVATORS (2.5%)
EARLY ADOPTERS (13.5%)
EARLY MAJORITY (34%)
LATE MAJORITY (34%)
LAGGARDS (16%)[11]

Everett Rogers had gotten lost trying to persuade the right people with the wrong approach. He had tried to approach every farmer the same way instead of using different approaches for farmers with different needs and risk profiles. Focusing on innovators is critical when you're first getting a new idea off the ground. But getting solid market adoption means focusing on each group in turn.

Rogers' contemporary tech innovator and consultant, Geoffrey Moore, took it a step further. In his book *Crossing the Chasm: Marketing and Selling High-Tech Products to Mainstream Customers*, Moore shared that getting visionaries (the innovators and early adopters) to join you is actually the *easiest* step.

The most *difficult* step is when you are "crossing the chasm" between the bold visionaries (innovators and early adopters) who jump in early and those darn pragmatists (the early and late majority and laggards) who see jumping on your bandwagon as riskier.

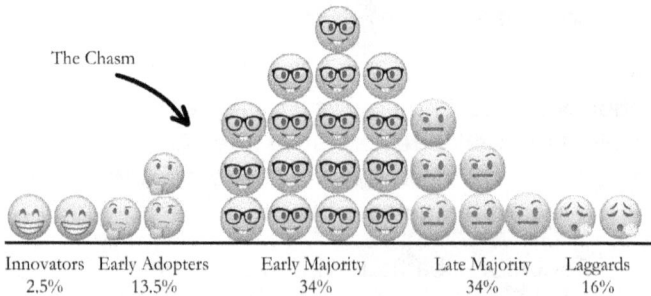

The Market Adoption Curve
Based on research by Everett Rogers and Geoffrey Moore[12]

The hard truth is that getting people to adopt your new idea requires that you address the needs of each group and recognize each one's unique differences and preferences.

Why does this matter?

When driving adoption for a high-stakes strategy, it's not about *you* and your vision. It's about *them*—your team, investors, customers, backers, and everyone else—and how comfortable *they* are adopting a new way of doing things.

Leaders often miss this point and are baffled when others don't get it. They can become impatient, frustrated, and even angry when people don't immediately join them. When you get frustrated with people, you lose momentum and can get lost. When you get lost on a trip, a "You Are Here" signpost helps you get your bearings. The same is true when driving your new strategy.

Where are *They* in the Market Adoption Journey?

If you're struggling to get people to join you as you execute your strategy, step back and look for signposts. I call this process of understanding who you are striving to reach the Market Adoption Journey. Thinking through this objectively keeps your focus clear—and on *them*. So ask yourself: Which people, which target groups, and which markets will bring the best results? And where are *they* on the Market Adoption Journey?

> *When you are driving adoption for a high-stakes strategy, it's not about YOU. It's about THEM.*

Consider these situations:

- *If you're a start-up:* Are you staying laser-focused on the visionaries—the innovators and early adopters—who are ready to say yes faster? Or are you spending tons of time doing dog-and-pony shows for anybody who has money and will talk to you?

- *If you're striving to cross the chasm:* Have you adapted your approach to be relevant to the pragmatists? Are you ready with the data, references, implementation plans, stories, and proof points they will need to feel comfortable taking risks with you? Or are you still using the same high-level razzle-dazzle pitch deck and demos you used for the visionaries?

- *If you have an established market:* Are you striving to stay relevant, continually listening to your customers' evolving needs and refining your marketing and sales approaches? Are you making sure those who already work with you feel appreciated?

Every audience is important, and each one will need *different* things from you. Plan for it. Don't get lost trying to convince people at various stages of the adoption journey by using the wrong approach at the wrong time with the wrong people.

With a little research and planning, you can target the *right* groups for the *right* stage of your strategy, especially if you anticipate the impact of change.

CHAPTER 6

THE POWER OF TRANSITION

The data was inescapable. The dashboard of key metrics was a sea of red. I'd been called in because the leadership team was stuck. Their high-stakes program was not going as fast as they had committed, and they were frustrated:

> "We told everyone this was urgent!"

> "We've got too many tree-huggers."

> "I think we need a new incentive plan. Let's get them in their wallets!"

These leaders were ready to blame everyone else for not changing fast enough. Yet they hadn't considered that adopting a new mindset takes time.

When you ask people to participate in your new high-stakes strategy, you are inviting them on a Transition Mindset Journey.

To successfully usher someone into this journey, it's essential to understand the difference between *change* and *transition*:

- *Change* happens to us, even if we don't agree with it. It could be a new set of tools or processes, a new regulation, a merger or acquisition, or a new market entry. It is external.

- *Transition* is internal. It's what happens within our minds as we deal with change. Change can happen very quickly, but transition occurs more slowly, and it is all about *mindset*.

Every single person you want to join your new strategy will have to go through a transition. Some will shift faster than others, but everyone will go through it, including you! You're just ahead of them.

Phases of Transition

William Bridges, an organizational change expert, saw this transition firsthand when he was struggling to come to terms with the emotional upheaval of his divorce. He reflected on his own experience and then did research with hundreds of individuals and organizations. In his book *Managing Transitions: Making the Most of Change*, Bridges observed that there are three phases of transition every human being has to go through.

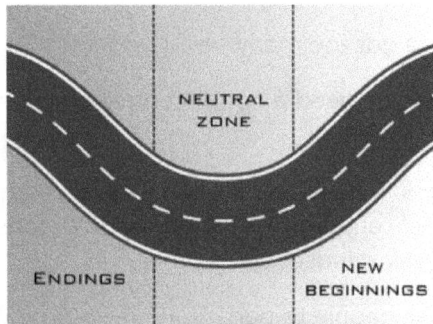

The Bridges Transition Model
Based on research by William Bridges[13]

Phase 1: ENDINGS

This phase is about letting go of the old. Sometimes letting go of something is simple. But sometimes it can be emotional: shock, fear, denial, sadness, or frustration. People have to accept that something is ending before they can accept something new. Even if they like some aspects of the new approach, there will inevitably also be changes they don't like.

People tend to fear what they don't understand. You can help at this stage by educating people about why the old way is no longer effective and how they might personally benefit from a change. When people understand the positive aspects of the future approach and how they can play an essential part in getting to that future, they are more likely to want to move to the next phase.

Phase 2: THE NEUTRAL ZONE

This is the bridge between the old and the new, where people are less attached to the old but still not clear what this "new" phase is all about. They may also be having to work harder than they're used to. Learning new systems, tools, and processes takes more energy, and that can be frustrating. In this phase, you need to expect a *productivity dip* from executing a new strategy!

But you can seize this moment as a leader. Though they may still come across as skeptical, people in this neutral phase start to listen a little bit more easily. They start to understand the outcome and their role in it. (But don't expect them to tell you that they are excited about it yet!)

Phase 3: NEW BEGINNINGS

When people build new skills and work in new ways that improve how they get things done, they will start to see early wins. The wins may be small, but new beginnings bring *hope*. In this phase, people are likely to feel a little relief and become even more open to listening and learning. It is also the phase where people will more openly talk about their experiences and bring others along with them.

Leading Through Transition

Your job as a leader is to ensure your key people don't get "lost in transition." Knowing where you and your organization are in this transition process will help you lead more compassionately. Every phase is important to translating your big idea into reality.

Consider the following questions:

- *Which transition phase are YOU in personally?* Have you let go of the old approach? Or are you in the neutral zone, adjusting to the new strategy but still needing to fully embrace the new ways of doing things? Be honest! Your own fearful or skeptical mindset will show as you lead others, despite the official game face you may be wearing. This can create a ripple effect of uncertainty and delay others' willingness to take action. Acknowledging that you are on a transition journey—just like everyone else—can help build credibility and trust.

- *What about your leadership team? Your board?* Are they talking a good game but unwilling to change themselves? Openly discuss where each leader and board member is currently and what they will need to do differently to "walk the walk" of your high-stakes strategy. You will not only speed results by getting more aligned, but these leaders will have more empathy for those on the front lines doing the heavy lifting. When your leaders better understand what your team is going through, they'll also start building more realistic timelines and accurately assessing the capacity of your organization to produce results while going through significant transitions.

- *What phase of transition are your managers and front line going through?* Even if they've gone through all sorts of training, these folks may still be in the neutral zone: resigned to the need for change but exhausted by the learning curve. Instead of seeing people as pushing back on your perfect strategy, take the time to understand where people are struggling most and consider their recommendations. Demonstrate that you respect what people are going through and that you are *listening* to what they're feeling. Simply sharing your own challenges can build TRUST and help others get more comfortable taking new steps forward.

- *Beyond your own organization, what about partners, suppliers, customers, and members?* The success of your high-stakes strategy also depends on individuals who do *not* work for you. Don't look at them as companies—think of them as *people!* Consider ways to anticipate everyone's transition journey and make a plan to support them at each phase. Consider how the change will impact their organization and identify ways to navigate the most challenging aspects.

Remember, despite how loyal they are, people don't take action if it is solely for the benefit of an *organization*. Make sure you clarify the benefits of taking action—whether it is peace of mind or the satisfaction that comes from being part of something bigger—for people as *individuals*.

As you lead people to achieve a high-stakes strategy, you are not simply setting objectives and hitting milestones. Like the captain of a ship, you are planning the voyage so your valuable passengers don't get lost in transition.

Congratulations!

You are ready to create momentum with your own ACCELERATION ADVANTAGE™. You understand the context for your efforts and are prepared to stay the course as you progress along the Strategy Process Journey, the Market Adoption Journey, and the Transition Mindset Journey. You have a better idea of where you are today and have gained insights about what's ahead.

The rest of this book will introduce specific ways to fast track your strategy and lead more confidently. You are in the driver's seat. Now it's time to make sure you're ready—starting with identifying the risks.

Section 2 Key Takeaways
Creating Your ACCELERATION ADVANTAGE™

You can move your strategy faster when you are intentional about creating an ACCELERATION ADVANTAGE™. But as you lead others in a new direction, it's important to be clear about where you are and where you are going.

- Leveraging the ACCELERATION ADVANTAGE™, you will create momentum by consistently

  - *De-risking your strategy* to avoid common mistakes

  - *Aligning people* to reduce the friction

  - *Communicating* to move people to action and speed results

  - *Adapting* continually to create windows of opportunity and seize them faster.

  In doing so, you are creating a powerful flywheel to speed and sustain your strategy.

- Implementing a successful strategy is a *process*. Skipping stages of the Strategy Process will actually slow down results.

- To get people to adopt your new idea, you must address the *right people* at the *right time* with the *right approach*. Market Adoption is not about you and your vision. It's about *them* and helping people get comfortable adopting a new way of doing things.

- Every person experiencing change must go through a *mindset transition* to move forward. When you recognize and support the phase of the Transition Mindset they are in, people will join you more quickly.

Section 2 Notes and Action Steps
Creating Your Own ACCELERATION ADVANTAGE™

(Jot down two to three things that jumped out that you can quickly apply.)

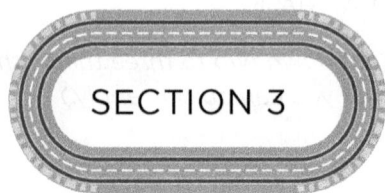

SECTION 3

GET IN GEAR: DE-RISKING YOUR STRATEGY FOR IMPACT

Take calculated risks. That is quite different from being rash.
George Patton, Olympic pentathlete and
World War II Allied military leader

How you prepare for a high-speed car race can determine whether you win or lose:

> Is the technology able to perform consistently at 200 miles per hour?

> Is your pit crew ready to service the car in thirteen seconds flat?

> Do you know the unique twists and turns of this course?

> Are your skills honed to maneuver within inches of cars in every direction?

In much the same way, as you drive your new strategy, there is a lot you need to plan for to ensure you're positioned to succeed. In Section 3, we will dive into an issue that will make or break your strategy: how you plan for and navigate *risk*.

In Chapters 7, 8, and 9, you'll explore your relationship with risk and why it's important to address the risks of your strategy openly and regularly. You'll also consider the underlying assumptions you're making and why getting clear up front about what you are assuming can help you avoid false starts.

In Chapters 10 and 11, you'll be introduced to "de-risking." You will learn the key principles of the DE-RISK SYSTEM FOR IMPACT®, a powerful system I developed specifically to help you identify and navigate the risks of your strategy.

Every racing team has a detailed checklist to ensure their car is ready. In much the same way, as you go through Section 3, you'll have the opportunity to work through what you need to do to address the risks of your strategy and lead more confidently.

CHAPTER 7
YOUR RELATIONSHIP WITH RISK

A ship in harbor is safe, but that's not what ships are for.
John Augustus Shedd, professor and author

Let's play a word association game. What comes to mind when you see this word?

RISK

When it comes to *risk*, most people immediately think of something to be avoided at all costs. It might be the risk of a natural disaster, like a fire or a flood. Or they might think about human risk, such as a car accident or a heart attack. In the marketplace, many people think risk is all about losing assets: money, customers, or your reputation.

Like it or not, risk is at the center of all decision making. New strategies are often about placing big bets, and there are a lot of unknowns with upside risk and downside risk. A long time ago, I realized that if we are going to galvanize support and increase the chances that a new strategy will work, we need to talk about risk. Yet I frequently see people avoiding it.

I've worked alongside countless cross-functional teams that struggled with confronting the risks of their strategy head-on. The stress was palpable. It showed up in snippy conversations, missed commitments, and blame. These teams would miss windows of opportunity or encounter pitfalls that could have been avoided—or at least recovered from faster—if they'd just been able to talk about the risks openly and objectively.

Then there are the senior leaders I've worked with who are actually very comfortable *taking risks*, yet they don't necessarily like to talk about risk either! They may be enthusiastic about all the possibilities but somehow feel that talking about risk is a downer. These gifted leaders have a big vision and tend to see risks as a normal part of doing business. Yet they often struggle to see the "people side of risk" to their strategy. They are often surprised when others don't share their excitement. They misjudge the challenges of getting people to take action and often underestimate the confusion and skepticism of employees, partners, suppliers, and customers.

I've found that executing a new strategy is easier when you use a proactive, systematic approach to discussing risk. By anticipating risks up front, you encourage problem-solving, enable teams to come up with creative solutions before problems arise, and help people adapt more quickly when they run into roadblocks.

For all of these reasons, I designed the DE-RISK SYSTEM FOR IMPACT® to help leaders navigate risk more effectively. We'll discuss the principles of the system later in this section, but it all starts with talking about risk.

What Is Risk?

Let's be clear about what we mean by risk. I define risk this way:

> *Risk: (noun) An unknown, a lack of information about the future. The result can be positive or negative, and sometimes both.*

Since the beginning of time, humans have known that bad things can happen. We've always needed to be ready with a Plan B or even a Plan C and Plan D!

When we consider the negative side of risk, our challenge is to ensure that we do all we can to *protect value and avoid loss.*

But there is another side to risk. We are willing to live with a negative outcome if it means we could achieve a positive one. When we make investments in stocks or real estate, we accept the risk that we might lose something in hopes of gaining an even greater financial return. A construction worker risks possible injury on a busy construction site but considers the risk worthwhile in exchange for the opportunity to earn income for her family.

When we anticipate this positive side of risk, the challenge is to *create more value* than we started with. It requires being prepared to quickly seize windows of opportunity with our eyes wide open, ready to take action.

Your Relationship with Risk Makes a Difference

The Biblical story of the Parable of the Talents offers insight into how people's decisions can be influenced by their attitudes about risk. If this parable were updated for today, it would be the story of a successful entrepreneur who entrusts three employees with some of his own money before going on a long trip. He gives one employee the equivalent of a year's salary, five months' salary to the second employee, and two months' salary to the third.

When he gets back from his trip, the entrepreneur asks the employees, "What were you able to accomplish with what I gave you?" The employee who was given a year's salary put his money to work in investments and doubled it. The second employee bought and sold an asset and also doubled his funds. To these two, the entrepreneur says, "Well done."

But the third guy was *frozen!* The uncertainty was overwhelming: "What to do? This is so risky! What if I lose the money? I'll be in trouble! My boss might be angry! I know, I'll take the safe bet. I'll hide the money under my bed."

This third employee probably felt relieved he hadn't lost any money. But it turns out that this wise entrepreneur's whole point was to encourage his employees to step up and learn how to take a risk *with* him! He had empowered each of his employees to make their best decision with the resources they'd been given and the lessons he had taught them. It was *their relationships with risk* that resulted in their making very different decisions.

Growing up, I was always fascinated by this parable and the insights it provides about risk-taking and faith. It prompts so many questions, it could have been a full-length movie! What made this wise entrepreneur so generous that he trusted his employees and was willing to share part of his hard-earned money? What if the first two guys had made the exact same investments but "failed fast"? And what happened to the third guy earlier in his life that made him so fearful about taking risks?

Your Relationship with Risk Is Complex

Your own relationship with risk affects how you make decisions every day.

Michele Wucker, author of *You Are What You Risk: The New Art and Science of Navigating an Uncertain World*, frames several types of risk personalities. Are you

- *Risk-Seeking*, with a tendency to prefer risks, all other things being equal?

- *Risk Averse*, with a tendency to avoid risks, all other things being equal?

- *Risk Savvy*, able to recognize and assess dangers and opportunities while balancing emotion and reason, taking smart precautions?[14]

Many different factors impact our relationship with risk. For instance, past experiences shape our views. Children who grew up during the Great Depression, after the stock market crash in 1929, learned that there are serious consequences if you don't have enough money for food and basics. Those who grew up during the "Go-Go" 1960s or in the abundance of the 21st century have a hard time relating to frugal grandparents who insist on repairing old appliances instead of buying new ones.

Countries have unique risk profiles too. Gallup and Lloyd's Register Foundation produces the World Worry Index.

Surveying 125,000 participants from 121 countries, the index indicates which countries worry the most and the least. Mali, a small country in northwestern Africa, emerged as the most worried country, while Sweden, in the Nordic region, worried the least.[15] Just as in the case of the Parable of the Talents, these differing perspectives invite us to consider the experiences and culture of people in these countries that shape their different views about risk.

An Organization's Risk Profile

Just as countries have different risk profiles, organizations have their own cultures and view risk differently. Leaders in bold, disruptive start-ups are often more comfortable doing whatever it takes and winging it to secure that first new customer. On the other hand, leaders in more mature, established firms with thousands of employees and legacy customer relationships tend to view risk more cautiously.

When you mix individual risk profiles, organizational risk cultures, and country risk cultures together, it can be a wild ride! I was once part of a merger of two global companies comprised of a myriad of cultural playbooks. Picture this: a launch team comprised of people from the United States and the United Kingdom, Germany and Scandinavia, India and Brazil. Some team members had worked in their organizations for decades, while others had just joined us to add a little startup spice to the mix.

It was exciting—and exhausting! Our wide-ranging risk profiles regularly appeared during unending debates: Is this product really ready enough for trial? Are we overcommitting with this contract? Which word is more accurate to promote our offering?

Some of the more methodical Europeans clashed with impetuous North Americans, who preferred to cut to the chase with snappy taglines. Some team members who grew up in more formal, structured organizations insisted on layers of approval. Meanwhile, those with experience in flatter, fast-moving organizations were ready to strike big deals based on a single text! Navigating this quilt of risk profiles provided endless challenges and significant learnings about people as we shaped a new corporate culture.

When leading any team, it is important to respect people's differences. But when you are leading a new strategy in a multi-cultural, multi-organizational environment, you can unwittingly bring progress to a standstill by ignoring people's different risk profiles. If you want people to take action faster, start with understanding *and respecting* their relationship with risk.

Sometimes, that starts with taking a risk yourself.

CHAPTER 8

WHEN NOT TALKING ABOUT RISK IS RISKY

Have you ever left the theater feeling disoriented after seeing a movie about the future? Whether it's *The Matrix*, *Star Trek*, *Ex Machina*, or *WALL-E*, when a futuristic film ends, it can leave you in another world. You feel exhausted from the trip, and when you awkwardly step back into your day-to-day reality, you may feel disappointment or relief, depending on the nature of the story. But connecting the dots from the future to the real world can take an adjustment.

The same thing can happen when you consider the future of your strategy. Envisioning your organization's future can provide fascinating new insights that can be heart-pumping, inspiring, or even a little scary.

But when you leave the "future-thinking theatre" and are confronted with your current reality, the questions become, What can I do about that future *today*? How effectively will our strategy be able to deal with all these risks?

It's at this point that people often have a blind spot. Many leaders find it's more comfortable to wax eloquent about their future than to talk frankly about how they are going to manage the risks of getting there.

I get it. There are a variety of reasons why people might be uncomfortable talking about risk. For instance:

- *When there aren't easy answers, some leaders clam up.* They don't know what to say, so they say nothing.

The problem is people around them fill the silence with worst-case scenarios and fight-or-flight reactions. Anxiety reigns.

- *Some leaders choose a strategy based on their gut instincts.* But in their zeal, these leaders stop listening to other perspectives. Discussions of their strategy's risks are shut down. People are trampled by all the unspoken "elephants in the room" that no one feels comfortable talking about, and known problems never get addressed.

- *Some leaders need to have all the answers.* When asked what risks they see in their strategy, they quickly respond, "Don't worry. I've got it all handled," and try to close down all questions. The leader is like the captain of a ship claiming it's unsinkable, brushing off warnings about icebergs—until the ship hits one.

Not talking about risk creates its own problems.

Talking Openly About Risk

When you lead a strategy, there are three ways that talking about risk can help you speed results:

1. *Regularly talking about risk will reduce anxiety.*

   It might be counter-intuitive, but one of the best ways to eliminate anxiety in an organization is to address uncertainty and risk head-on. The more leaders openly talk about risk, the less powerful the anxiety becomes.

   Did you know that there is a psychological therapy that helps people achieve the same thing? Exposure and Response Prevention (ERP) Therapy encourages you to face your fears when confronted with anxiety, but only at a level you can tolerate. For example, if you're afraid of flying, you might start by just getting on the plane, sitting down, buckling your seat belt, and then getting off without ever actually leaving the ground. If that feels okay, next time, you might try a flight simulator or watch a movie about a flight.

Over time, patients learn that the thoughts and feelings that prompt distress are more bearable than they anticipated. The uncertainty that they worried so much about doesn't necessarily lead to the outcomes they feared.

As a leader, you can use this ERP concept to help your team anticipate challenges and plan for worst-case scenarios. You can turn elephant-in-the-room-sized nightmares into smaller, more manageable issues that just require a practical plan. Suddenly, a room full of people who were bogged down and struggling with their individual anxieties is instead united by a common task: making a plan to achieve a doable goal.

2.   *Openly talking about risk can help your organization shift gears faster.*

Talking about risk can reduce anxiety, help your organization shift gears faster, and create a competitive advantage.

When you regularly discuss the possible risks ahead, people who once needed all the answers become a little more comfortable developing "minimum viable" game plans for different scenarios. They become less rigid about finding one perfectly right answer.

Morale improves as people realize their concerns are being heard. Anxiety dissipates. If you and your leaders are comfortable with uncertainty yourselves, your team can get more comfortable too. You can break down silos and make collaboration easier when people feel safe talking about the implications of risk and start to view it with a wider lens.

3.   *Acknowledging and planning for risk can create a competitive advantage.*

Recognizing changes around you and openly discussing risks can open doors to new opportunities. When people get comfortable coming up with different ways to address disruption, they start to develop more flexible decision-making muscles. They not only react more quickly but are able to seize windows of opportunity faster than the competition.

This ability to stretch your thinking and make decisions in the face of risk can become a differentiator for your organization. While other organizations may freeze at the disruption around them, yours can thrive. As your team becomes more comfortable with uncertainty, they become like race car drivers navigating through traffic, seeing openings and opportunities to advance, and making quick, calculated moves to turn challenges into progress.

If you want to reduce anxiety, help your organization shift gears faster, or create a competitive advantage, talking about risk is essential. It will help you move your strategy forward, lead with your eyes open, and enable your organization to thrive.

You can start by understanding the assumptions you're making and whether or not they are true.

CHAPTER 9

THE POWER AND THE
TRAP OF ASSUMPTIONS

Your assumptions are your windows on the world.
Scrub them off every once in a while, or the light won't come in.
Alan Alda, actor, director, and author

We were going over the sales results, and emotions in the room were running high. "It's obvious why we're in this mess," the sales leader grumbled. "I *assumed* we would be able to deliver what we promised."

The head of product development snapped back, "Well, I *assumed* you would sell the product roadmap we agreed to instead of making it up and overpromising!" The room fell into a tense silence, each person feeling the weight of disappointment.

When I work with teams trying to get a high-stakes strategy back on track, there is often a lot of stress. The frustration is usually rooted in the fact that they have made *very different assumptions* that led them to *very different conclusions*. Often, they had never even stopped to consider their assumptions. They launched a new strategy with lots of excitement but just assumed things would turn out well.

Why This Matters

An assumption is a statement that is accepted to be true without proof. We all make assumptions every day. We assume that the sun will rise in the morning, that our car will start without issues, and that our client will like the green letterhead better than the blue one.

But which assumptions are true? And which ones aren't? Defining your assumptions and proving them true (or false!) early on can help you anticipate and navigate the unknowns of your strategy.

Have You Written Down Your Assumptions?

Your assumptions shape your lens for looking at a problem. They shape your questions as well as your answers. Yet many leadership teams make the mistake of jumping into problem-solving without ever taking the time to openly and objectively state what they are assuming.

Getting clear about your assumptions requires intentionally stepping back and asking yourself bigger questions. "What is causing me to believe that this is true?" and "What am I assuming about the people, the marketplace, or the way things work in the world that would lead to this conclusion?"

For instance, when you launch a new offering, you might be assuming:

- Customers will want to spend money on this solution.
- Our suppliers will be able to meet our timelines.
- Our own organization will understand and be able to explain our offering.
- These price points are competitive.
- We can create enough revenue to cover our costs.
- Our competition cannot easily match this offering.

If you're launching an important internal initiative, you might be assuming:

- Everyone we know agrees that this problem is important and it needs to be solved right now.
- The people who have to implement this change understand why we are taking this approach.

- Our people have the capacity to implement this change.

- Everyone involved in this initiative will easily adopt the new approach.

- The outcome we intend will be seen quickly.

Some assumptions are less obvious, and you'll need to dig deeper. Data buried in a spreadsheet can reflect assumptions you didn't even realize you were making, especially if someone else is running the numbers!

How Do You Know Your Assumptions Are True?

Our normal habit as humans is to seek out information that supports our beliefs. Research shows that we tend to look for and remember information that validates that we're right. Psychologists call this "confirmation bias."

For instance, as you revel in your purchase of a new car, you might suddenly notice news stories and rave reviews from satisfied owners while ignoring any negative articles. If you've heard negative things about a particular city, you might automatically avoid visiting without considering that your own experience might be different.

It's important to actively seek diverse perspectives to challenge your assumptions. You can start by simply typing "common assumptions and misconceptions about (the problem)" in your favorite search engine or artificial intelligence (AI) tool. Interview people on the front lines who have the problem you're trying to solve. Do some surveys and talk to experts. Approach the process with the mindset of a detective, rewarding yourself for uncovering insights that challenge your preconceptions.

Finding out early that your assumptions are *true* can build confidence in your plans. However, finding out early that your assumptions are *false* allows you to make critical course adjustments that can actually speed results. Getting clear on your assumptions will put you in a stronger position to manage the risks ahead.

CHAPTER 10

WHAT IS DE-RISKING AND WHY DOES IT MATTER?

When skilled race car drivers move at 200 miles an hour, they have to consider the risks of physical injuries, financial loss, and missed windows of opportunity as they maneuver to win. Their approach is intentional.

How you manage the risk of your strategy needs to be intentional as well.

De-risking can help. I define "de-risking" this way:

> *De-risking: (verb) A systematic process of identifying and optimizing risk to make decisions with more confidence and achieve desired outcomes.*

De-risking is a fast and furious game, and it applies to all sorts of industries:

- *911 operators* start de-risking the moment they become aware of an emergency. When a new distress call is sounded, they gather crucial information about the situation and assess the level of risk involved. They ask questions about the nature of the emergency, the location, and potential hazards or threats present.

- *Finance and insurance managers* de-risk their portfolios to make sure they've got enough assets to cover their obligations. Not complying with regulations can damage an institution's reputation, resulting in lost customers and serious penalties from regulators.

Being too cautious, on the other hand, can lead to an unintended bias against less developed neighborhoods and countries.

- *Software developers* proactively manage the risks of technology failures, "scope creep," budget overruns, and missed market windows. They de-risk against tech failures by testing their code, performing quality assurance tests, and debugging regularly. Clear project priorities and stakeholders' feedback help avoid expanding the project beyond its original goals. Market research, trend evaluation, and competitor research enable them to quickly adapt their development strategies to meet market windows.

People de-risk decisions every day to ensure they accomplish their goals. Thomas Stanton of Johns Hopkins University reminds us that risk management is not intended to create more bureaucracy but to facilitate discussion about big risks.[16] *The big risks are often the ones most worth taking!*

In de-risking conversations, the consequences and possibilities can be explored, and leaders can consciously apply their values to decision making. In doing so, they become more confident about the direction they are taking.

What approach do you and your team use today to discuss the risk of your new strategy? Do you have a way to consistently explore and manage different types of risks?

CHAPTER 11

YOUR ACCELERATION ADVANTAGE™: THE DE-RISK SYSTEM FOR IMPACT®

When you and your team proactively address risk, you can improve the likelihood your strategy will succeed. *But how do you tackle a conversation about risk?*

Discussing risk is not always comfortable, especially when risk involves people. When the subject is broached, the discussion can become accusatory, defensive, or cautious or simply come to a halt.

I realized we needed a new way to talk about risk—especially risk related to the people side of a strategy. Drawing from my own experience and research, I set out to develop a clear, actionable system using language that individuals from all backgrounds, industries, roles, and cultures could understand.

I distilled strategic business concepts that I found consistently worked into the principles of the DE-RISK SYSTEM FOR IMPACT®. These straightforward principles now serve as the foundation for my own consulting services. After applying them in hundreds of cases—large and small—I can definitely say that these principles directly result in improved outcomes and more confident teams.

Why You Need A System

I recall a frustrating meeting during a merger. The merging companies had different approaches to launching a new product, and senior leaders couldn't agree on the best method. After hours of debate, one exasperated employee finally stood up and said, "I don't care if we do it your way or if we do it our way or if we do it a new way. *Just tell me how we do things here* so I can do my job!"

In times of uncertainty, people are more willing to take action when expectations are clear. A system helps by setting expectations, prioritizing resources, and holding everyone accountable to move forward together.

In ride-sharing services like Uber and Lyft, both drivers and passengers rely on a system to ensure smooth, timely rides and avoid confusion. The Global Positioning System (GPS) provides real-time location, timing, and directional guidance to help people navigate challenges efficiently. Drivers use GPS to find passengers and calculate the best routes, accounting for traffic and road conditions, while passengers depend on it for reliable pickups and confident travel. The system creates consistency and reliability, ensuring everyone understands, *"This is how we do things here."*

A system for dealing with uncertainty as you define and execute your strategy works the same way. It helps everyone understand your big idea so they can do their part to deliver results. It helps everyone understand the risks and know how to manage it together. It's counterintuitive, but when you take the time up front to put a system in place for implementing your strategy and managing the risks, you'll get the results you want faster than if you'd rushed into execution.

The DE-RISK SYSTEM FOR IMPACT®

One of the four success factors of your ACCELERATION ADVANTAGE™ is to *de-risk* your strategy. The principles of the DE-RISK SYSTEM FOR IMPACT® can help you get results faster by:

- Systematically uncovering the hidden risks of your new strategy

- Developing a game plan to manage those risks

- More confidently helping others to acknowledge risk and take action.

What makes this approach different?

The DE-RISK SYSTEM FOR IMPACT® proactively addresses the *people* side of risk, which can derail even the *best* strategy.

The ACCELERATION ADVANTAGE™
Go to Market Impact LLC

Clients tell me after using this system that it stands out from others because it

- Enables people to talk about risk openly and productively

- Is based on concepts that make sense and are easy to understand and apply, no matter your role, your industry, your culture, or the stage or size of your organization

- Complements other methodologies you may use for strategic planning, risk management, launch introduction, or program and project management

- Provides practical tools your team can start using immediately.

In a surprisingly short period of time you can apply these principles and more confidently lead people to take action.

De-risking is best implemented as a team that is comprised of people from different functions, backgrounds, and demographics. By seeking diverse perspectives, you can examine the key components of your strategy from every angle, gaining insights you would have otherwise missed.

Be prepared to be vulnerable. De-risking demands that you become more transparent and share more openly how you feel about risk than you may have ever done in the past.

WARNING: The principles of the Dᴇ-Rɪsᴋ Sʏsᴛᴇᴍ ꜰᴏʀ Iᴍᴘᴀᴄᴛ® sound deceptively simple! Yet some of the biggest organizations in the world, and many organizations with very compelling missions, have stumbled, stalled, or completely failed because they underestimated the importance of these principles. *Skip them at your own peril!*

(Download a copy of the Dᴇ-Rɪsᴋ Sʏsᴛᴇᴍ ꜰᴏʀ Iᴍᴘᴀᴄᴛ® principles at bonus.fasttrackyourbigidea.com.)

The Principles of the Dᴇ-Rɪsᴋ Sʏsᴛᴇᴍ ꜰᴏʀ Iᴍᴘᴀᴄᴛ®

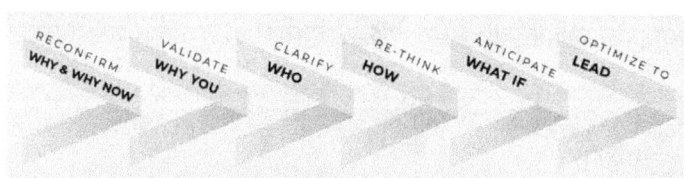

The Dᴇ-Rɪsᴋ Sʏsᴛᴇᴍ ꜰᴏʀ Iᴍᴘᴀᴄᴛ®

Principle 1: Rᴇᴄᴏɴꜰɪʀᴍ Wʜʏ ᴀɴᴅ Wʜʏ Nᴏw

Focusing on the solution without confirming the problem you are solving results in confusion. Framing the problem and the consequences of not solving it creates urgency.

Principle 2: Vᴀʟɪᴅᴀᴛᴇ Wʜʏ Yᴏᴜ

People have options. Be able to articulate what makes you unique. It will help you be seen and heard.

Principle 3: Cʟᴀʀɪꜰʏ Wʜᴏ

To make a meaningful impact, you need people to help. Don't underestimate all those who need to take action. Understand why they would be willing to do something new.

Principle 4: Rᴇ-Tʜɪɴᴋ Hᴏw

You may need to leverage different approaches as you solve the problem over time. To avoid surprises, anticipate the impact on your business model and on the Decision Makers' Journey.

Principle 5: ANTICIPATE WHAT IF

Obstacles and opportunities will arise. Continually thinking through risks and scenarios helps your team move faster and smarter and builds confidence.

Principle 6: OPTIMIZE TO LEAD

Leading through change requires a risk-savvy culture and leaders who are intentional about growing personally.

Exploring the Principles of De-Risking

Throughout this chapter, we'll examine each of the six principles of the DE-RISK SYSTEM FOR IMPACT®. (Heads up: This section is a little longer than the others, but I promise it's worth it!)

You'll be challenged with specific questions to consider for your own strategy. While you go through each principle, start jotting down your thoughts and specific actions you can take today. Capture the assumptions you are making and the risks you will need to manage.

When I hold de-risking programs with clients, I challenge every member of the team to work through these ideas independently first and document their thinking. Only then do we bring people together to compare notes. That way, every individual goes through their own thinking process. We benefit from every perspective, especially from those whose quieter voices are often not heard.

Some clients tell me that de-risking their strategy took longer than expected. When I ask why, the answer is always the same: "The questions are simple. It's the *thinking* that takes time!"

De-risking isn't complicated, but it demands that you thoughtfully examine the basis for your strategy. There may be familiar principles that you have overlooked and some you've never considered before.

By investing time to reflect and discuss your thinking with your team, you'll establish the underpinnings for your strategy. This can help you align more quickly and stay aligned down the road.

Taking the time to carefully consider risks will build your organization's de-risking muscles. By documenting assumptions, exploring "what if" scenarios, and testing ideas before committing resources, you're not just protecting this strategy—you're creating a repeatable approach that becomes *how we do it here* for all future initiatives. Your team will develop the habit of pausing to ask, "What are we missing? What would make this fail?" That discipline helps avoid blind spots even as markets, technologies, or stakeholder needs evolve.

This also accelerates learning. Your team can review past de-risking sessions to see which risks materialized, which didn't, and how well your mitigation plans worked. This turns every strategy effort into a learning loop that makes the organization smarter and more adaptable. In a world where change is constant, the ability to learn and adjust quickly is one of the greatest competitive advantages you can build.

Ready to get started?

DE-RISK SYSTEM FOR IMPACT®
PRINCIPLE 1

RECONFIRM WHY AND WHY NOW: YOUR FUEL TO ACCELERATE RESULTS

A foundational element of your strategy is your vision, your WHY. This is the problem you are solving, your purpose, your cause, your beliefs—the reason you exist and why anyone should care. Your WHY is the fuel that will help you plan and launch your new strategy and sustain it for the long run.

The Power of a Clear WHY

You are probably familiar with author Simon Sinek and his powerful book *Start with Why: How Great Leaders Inspire Everyone to Take Action*. Simon challenges us: "People don't buy what you do; they buy why you do it. What you do simply proves what you believe."[17] Inspired purpose-led organizations make sure they are clear about their WHY, not just their *what*.

But what Simon Sinek failed to point out is that being clear about your WHY can also help you navigate more effectively when things get bumpy. Getting clear about your WHY (the problem you solve) instead of the details of *how* you solve it, can help you see new options more easily despite the disruption. When you are laser-focused on your purpose, you can more easily shift your thinking when you run into roadblocks. You can accomplish your WHY in new ways that may ultimately serve your larger mission even better!

A clear WHY also helps you be less fearful about risk. The mother who flees a war-torn country with only the shirt on her back sees risk in the context of her bigger purpose: to ensure the survival of her children. Hopefully, your risks are a little less scary for you. But when we know our WHY, we can make better, more informed decisions in our own lives and for our team.

In an uncertain environment, WHY serves as your compass. But there's another question you need to answer: Is what we are doing relevant *today*?

The Urgency of WHY NOW

In a dynamic world, what was important yesterday may be irrelevant today. If the problem you solve (or the opportunity you are trying to create) has lost its relevance, there will be no urgency. There are lots of things that might make the world a little bit better—someday. But people aren't willing to spend their time or money without a sense of urgency.

To engage people to take action, make sure you are prepared to answer the question, *Why does this specific problem need to be solved—now?* Consider the following:

- What current trends are impacting this problem? Are they making this problem more or less urgent to solve?

- How has the scale or scope of this problem changed?

- Are there any recent events that have made this problem more visible?

- How have public perceptions about this problem changed?

- Are there new audiences who need this problem solved?

The Cost of Inaction

Another way to determine WHY NOW is to understand the consequences of *not* solving the problem! Some people may believe things will "work out over time." Providing facts about the real-world consequences of *not* taking action can motivate people to step up and take action faster.

Deepti Arora recognized the power of articulating the *cost of inaction*. In the midst of a merger, when management was focused on finding synergies and reducing costs, Deepti challenged the senior leaders of Nokia with a big idea: the Cost of Quality.

"Imagine the savings if we addressed even half of our quality problems earlier. Instead of resolving them in the field, we can catch them before they get out the door. How can we afford to overlook costs that could be in the millions? What if we quantified the consequences of losing customer trust? Can we afford to wait?" Deepti, who was appointed Nokia's Chief Quality Officer, ignited a fire within the leadership team and harnessed the momentum. By challenging these leaders to consider the *cost of inaction*, Deepti helped the organization embrace quality faster as a strategic priority and competitive edge.

Taking the time to explore WHY NOW and framing the consequences of inaction creates an urgency that can't be ignored.

Making More Informed Decisions

Once you've evaluated WHY NOW, you can make better decisions.

- *If you find strong data to support* WHY NOW, enlist people with a more compelling call to action. Consequences are often more persuasive than promises.

- *If you cannot find objective data* proving the problem is urgent, do some research! The market may have moved, or people's priorities may be changing. In either case, research what *is* urgent to your target audience *now*. Put off any significant investment until you find people sincerely concerned about solving the problem you are so passionate about. Sometimes you can narrow your focus and find more support.

Clarifying your purpose with a clear WHY and WHY NOW will help you lead more effectively. It will also build the confidence of customers, funders, partners, and employees who see that you are focused on an important issue and ready to devise different ways to solve it.

Creating Your Own "Why/Why Now" Statement

Can you articulate your Why and Why Now so that others understand it? This doesn't have to be overly complicated. In fact, it can be stated in just a few sentences! The following is a simple formula I've found works well when you are trying to clarify Why and Why Now. Even if you think everyone seems to get it, you can use this exercise to reconfirm that your whole team sees your strategy the same way.

In helping people develop a concise way to explain Why, it is important to do this in steps. Start by having everyone think about this independently. Only after everyone has thought through their own views should you bring people together to talk about it. Whether it's your leadership team, board, project team, or committee, they each need to grapple with their understanding of Why/Why Now and come up with their own point of view.

When you come together for a discussion, you will be surprised to see how varied the perspectives can be. *If people are in complete disagreement, your strategy is at risk.*

Explore the underlying assumptions that are leading people to such different views. Assign homework to validate their different perspectives with objective data. If your team can come to a common understanding, it will be easier to execute together successfully.

You'll likely find that individuals will have captured different *dimensions* of the problem and its outcomes. They will see it from different angles due to their functional roles or life experiences.

Consider these insights as gems. They provide depth, clarity, and nuance as you define your Why. These insights can also help you relate to others who need to be part of your journey.

By getting clear about Why and Why Now, you've reduced one of the most significant risks for your strategy. People will understand what you're striving to achieve and why it is urgent. Their next question will be, "Why would I want to join *YOU*?"

YOUR WHY/WHY NOW FORMULA

This simple formula can help you frame the answers to WHY *and* WHY NOW *for your strategy. Download a template for this formula at bonus.fasttrackyourbigidea.com.*

Step 1: WHY

- The problem we solve is *(pain point)*

- for *(your target audiences)*

- to achieve *(the outcome that resolves this problem).*

Step 2: WHY NOW

- This problem is important to solve NOW because *(list the compelling reasons).*

- If this problem is NOT solved, the consequences are *(list the consequences).*

DE-RISK SYSTEM FOR IMPACT®
PRINCIPLE 2

VALIDATE WHY YOU: DIFFERENTIATING YOURSELF IN A COMPLEX WORLD

If you want others to join you to achieve your big idea, there is a simple question you need to be able to answer: *WHY YOU?*

People have options about where they invest their time, talent, and resources. Whether you're talking to potential customers, funders, employees, members, or volunteers, they want to know how you are different from others. My research has found that the most common advice from funders is this: *make sure you're very clear on why you're different—your niche.*

Jeff Grubb is an investment banker, management consultant, and now a trustee for the MJ Murdock Charitable Trust based in Vancouver, Washington. His view? "Despite what people may think, there is actually a lot of funding available for good ideas. But whether they lead a business or a nonprofit, most people looking for funding don't spend enough time asking themselves, 'Why do we exist?,' 'Why do we need one more organization doing this?,' 'Why is what we are doing going to be any different from others doing something like it?'"

Allison Schulz is Vice President of Capacity Building at the Calgary Foundation, a philanthropic organization working to build a healthy, vibrant community in Canada. When nonprofits come to her requesting funding, she says, "I encourage organizations to consider, 'What vacant spot would there be if we didn't do this work?,' 'Why is this work going to be important to the people we serve?,' 'Is this critical to do now? If not, when will it be?'"

If you don't define a clear niche for your organization, no matter how important your mission is, you won't get heard in this very noisy world. Your strategy will falter.

To clarify WHY YOU, take these two steps:

1. *Identify the gaps.*

   Make a list of all the organizations and people in your ecosystem. Who else is tackling the same problem from a different angle? There may be a lot of organizations in the same space using similar buzzwords. But when you dig into the details, you often find they are doing something a little different or coming at the problem in a different way.

   Do you see any *white space*? Gaps in the marketplace are opportunities to seize a unique niche. Organizations doing work related to your niche also represent opportunities for partnerships.

   For example, when Ana Maria Lowry, an international lawyer from Colombia, came to the United States to pursue a new career, she noticed a gap. Large corporations and government agencies wanted to hire diverse suppliers but struggled to find qualified companies that could deliver what they promised. Eager small business owners overpromised and were unprepared to meet the demanding standards of larger organizations. Ana Maria had a big idea: why not bridge the gap? She founded A&P International, a company that helps corporations and government agencies implement diverse supply chain initiatives more strategically. At the same time, they provide training and coaching for diverse small businesses to help them deliver higher value and compete more effectively. Creating new partnerships and a trusted ecosystem of diverse suppliers has become A&P International's unique niche.

   Getting a bigger picture of where you fit within a big market can be humbling. Many leaders struggle with this step. They may start off a little cocky ("We're the only ones on Earth doing this amazing thing!"), but once they study the market, they can end up depressed ("We sound like everyone else!").

That's when we go to the next step: exploring all the possible dimensions of your differentiation.

2. *Define what makes you different from every angle.*

If your *what* (your offering) is *truly* one-of-a-kind, clarifying WHY YOU should be easy. But what happens the day someone else comes up with something similar?

The good news is that your offering *is not* the only way you can differentiate. You can package or deliver your offering in a unique way, provide a unique experience, or serve a unique audience or geography. For instance:

- The founders of Warby Parker, students David Gilboa, Jeffrey Raider, and Andrew Hunt, believed everyone has the right to see. But they saw a problem: eyewear was too expensive. What if they could differentiate by *how they delivered* glasses? Their big idea was to make eyewear cheaper by creating a new way to reach their customers. They disrupted the market by selling directly to consumers, offering online and at-home trials, and lowering costs. For every pair sold, they donate one to someone in need through their Buy a Pair, Give a Pair program. Today, like so many DTC (Direct-to-Consumer) pioneers, they also have dozens of retail locations. However, they entirely reinvented the "try and buy" process and now claim millions of loyal customers and a $3 billion valuation.

- Amy & Ben Wright opened a coffee shop franchise in Wilmington, North Carolina. The Wrights call it "a human rights movement disguised as a coffee shop."[18] What sets Bitty & Beau's apart is *their people*. Their big idea was to create a place where people with disabilities are valued and given opportunities for meaningful work. Their stores, now franchised across the country, live out their mission every day and create a customer experience that keeps customers coming back. At least twice a day, they host dance parties and karaoke sing-alongs to liven things up!

These organizations realized that they could differentiate by leveraging their strengths in new ways. As you explore your own differentiation, take time to systematically list every strength you can think of. You are likely to find compelling evidence for WHY YOU that you and your team can genuinely believe in. Come up with one or two simple sentences to express WHY YOU that everyone can remember and share confidently.

Keep in mind as you do this important work: you're not only making it easier for people to buy into your vision. You're also building a more confident team that is clear and proud about what makes your organization exceptional!

DE-RISK SYSTEM FOR IMPACT®
PRINCIPLE 3

CLARIFY WHO: THE PEOPLE WHO NEED TO TAKE ACTION

The first-ever Formula 1 Grand Prix race took place in Turin, Italy, in 1946. For that first race to be a success, who had to take action? Your initial thought may be the drivers and the pit crews. But think more broadly! What about the investors and promoters of the event who had to fund a new race with a new set of rules? The people who worked in the restaurants and hotels in the area had to shift gears to be able to handle the crowds that day. And if no one had shown up in the stands for an entirely new type of competition that weekend, would the race have actually been a success?

Who Needs to Do Something New?

When it comes to executing a big new idea, *many* people have to be prepared and willing to do something new. That's why the De-Risk principle CLARIFY WHO is so important.

Many leaders make flawed assumptions about WHO. They underestimate the wide range of people, both inside and outside the organization, who need to be ready to make a change for the strategy to be successful.

Thinking through precisely WHO needs to take action is crucial. Start by mapping out all the people, roles, and organizations that must do something *new* for your strategy to be successful. You will want to make sure they're in the loop early. If they're surprised and confused by what you're asking them to do, your initiative will be delayed, if not derailed. You can think about WHO from two perspectives: internal and external.

Your *internal* Who includes (at least!):

- You
- Your leadership team
- Employees
- Contractors
- Partners
- Suppliers
- Volunteers
- Board members
- Funders
- Advisors

All of these people need to be informed, aligned, and ready to do their part. When your internal Who is informed early and clearly understands your new direction, they can bring their different perspectives and ideas to help you anticipate issues and get results faster. They need some notice if you want them to reprioritize to make time and capacity to support your initiative.

Your *external* Who is all those people you don't have as much control over but are critical to your success. Your *external* Who includes (at least!):

- Customers or members who may need to do things differently, such as changing their processes or training.

- Industry associations and consortia, ecosystem partners, and even competition who will need to play a part if you are striving to create a new industry standard or a movement.

- Community stakeholders who will need to fully understand what you are doing differently if they are going to recommend you to others or approve an exception.

- Beneficiaries who use your solution, even if others pay for it. These people will still have to understand that there is a change and be clear on what they need to do differently to be able to benefit.

Unfortunately, beneficiaries are often left out of the planning process, even by well-meaning organizations. Take, for instance, the challenge of providing clean water to remote areas of the world. According to the International Institute for Environment and Development, up to $360M was spent by donors and nongovernmental organizations to build water wells in rural Africa that ended up becoming useless over time. Why? Once the wells were drilled, the local community didn't have adequate funds to maintain the wells.

The nonprofit known as charity:water takes another approach. They work with local partners around the world right from the start to select where to create water points, ensuring community participation and planning for long-term sustainability. In addition to construction, local partners spend months ensuring the community understands the purpose of the well and is bought in, building the local capacity to manage and fund projects, as well as promoting safe hygiene practices so the water will remain clean.

When you plan ahead for Who needs to take action, you can avoid confusion and speed results. But do you know the one group that leaders most often forget when it comes to clarifying Who? *Themselves!* Leadership teams and boards need to consider how *they* will personally need to step up in new ways, or they can actually create risk for their strategy.

Be Specific About Taking Action

Once you are clear about Who needs to take action, the questions become "What do you want them to *do?*" and "Why would they *want* to do it?" People don't always move forward just because you tell them to! You'll need to do the work to help them understand, believe, and trust you enough to take action.

Senior executives and purpose-led leaders often make the mistake of expecting that because *they* think a significant change is necessary, *other* people will immediately get the idea and take action without much explanation. But that's not how humans work! People only take action when they understand the change and believe it makes sense. Without clarity, change can feel confusing and not worth the risk or inconvenience of changing the way they are doing things.

An inspired group of medical professionals I met with were committed to simplifying the complicated healthcare system. They founded a nonprofit, built a website, and were on their way—until they weren't. Excited supporters, initially inspired by the call to "create a movement," wanted more clarity. Without more details, interest began to wane.

Providing details about concrete actions you want people to take will help your audience grasp what you want them to do and do it faster, especially if you've considered a little brain science.

The Neuroscience of Taking Action

There are two sides of the brain. When your call to action includes lots of data and charts about what you want people to do, you're appealing to the *neocortex* part of the brain, which is responsible for people's rational and analytical thought and language.

But the *limbic brain*, often called the "old brain," is responsible for all of our feelings, like trust and loyalty. It's also responsible for behavior and decision making! Our limbic brain protects us. This is where the fight-or-flight response to fear is centered. To take a new action, our limbic brain needs to know WHY: *Why is doing this good for me? Is there a risk?*

When you take the time to ensure people understand the reasons for the change and how it benefits them, it will help them move beyond simply understanding to believing and trusting. It enables them to take the next step faster.

When you apply the CLARIFY WHO principle, make sure you wear your detective hat. As you start mapping all the people who need to take action for your strategy to be a success, you'll inevitably uncover people you might have otherwise skipped. This may take a little time, but doing this work early in your strategy process will accelerate results!

Download a worksheet to map out WHO needs to take action at bonus.fasttrackyourbigidea.com.

DE-RISK SYSTEM FOR IMPACT®
PRINCIPLE 4

RE-THINK HOW:
MAPPING THE JOURNEY

So far, you have identified several important building blocks of your strategy: WHY/WHY NOW, WHY YOU, and WHO. But to speed your strategy, you will need to be able to adjust your navigation as the journey unfolds. It's time to RE-THINK HOW to implement your big idea. This starts with a solid business model and a smooth road for the decision makers you want to join in.

Your Steering Wheel: A Balanced Business Model

When you are moving fast down a racetrack, all the moving parts of your automobile must work in balance. Otherwise, you will damage the engine and end up out of the race.

In the same way, a solid business model keeps your organization in balance so you can remain viable over time. To support your mission, there are two sides of your business model you need to plan for.

First, think of everything it takes to *create value*. If you ran a racetrack, you might think of these as your "off the track" activities you have to accomplish before the race even begins. You will need a plan for your offerings (products or services) to create a value proposition for others. You will also need resources to create those offerings (including people, materials, and technology). Think through the key activities needed to achieve your mission and the key processes that support those activities. And don't forget to plan for the funding required to cover all the costs!

Then, to balance your business model, you'll need a plan to *deliver value*. In our racing analogy, this is everything that happens "on the track," more visible to everyone watching the race. This includes the value proposition for the different audiences you serve and marketing channels to reach them (online, direct, resellers, etc.). And don't forget to plan for a way to fund your outreach!

Your business model is your map for balancing how you create and deliver value. Both sides can change and adapt over time; they just need to remain in balance.

One common mistake leaders make is to keep the business model a secret. When well-meaning employees, volunteers, or board members come up with new, innovative ideas, they get shut down with *Don't keep your business model a secret!* "we can't afford it" or "we don't have the resources." The boss quickly becomes the bad guy.

But when everyone on the team fully understands the business model, they can see the big picture across different functions. They can see the constraints and interdependencies along with you. This also helps them see where they fit in and can add value.

Instead of keeping it a secret, *educate your team about how your business model works!* Explain the elements that are most critical to making your organization viable. Explain how the budgets are built to address the costs and fund all the elements of the model.

When people come up with new ideas, don't shut them down! Encourage them to think through their idea and capture how they could fit into the business model. Once they have considered how to fund their initiative and how it will impact other parts of the model, you will be able to have a more meaningful discussion. In doing so, you will also be developing stronger leaders. Who knows what innovative, actionable ideas may come out of it.

A simple tool called a *Business Model Canvas* (BMC) can be very helpful when you're trying to visualize your new strategy. The BMC is a one-page document initially developed by Alexander Osterwalder and Yves Pigneur to help enthusiastic entrepreneurs explain their start-up ideas to investors on one page instead of using hundreds of PowerPoint slides. Now all types of organizations use it, from nonprofits to startups to Fortune 500 companies.

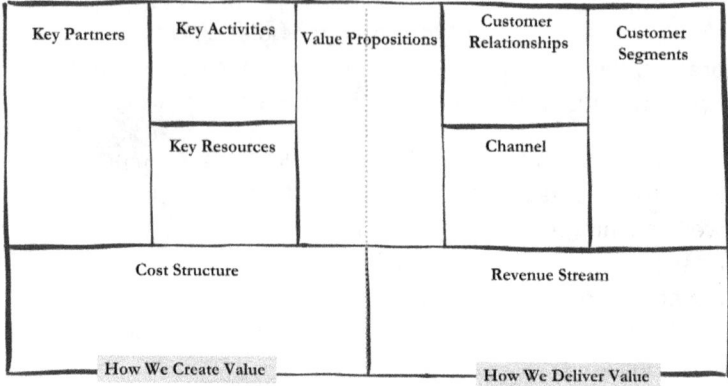

Key Partners	Key Activities	Value Propositions	Customer Relationships	Customer Segments
	Key Resources		Channel	

Cost Structure	Revenue Stream
——— How We Create Value	——— How We Deliver Value

The Business Model Canvas (BMC)
Developed by Osterwalder and Pigneur[19]

Each part of your business model affects the others. When you think about making a change, you can use the BMC to help you think through the implications across your model. You can find out more about the Business Model Canvas at bonus.fasttrackyourbigidea.com.

Inviting others to help you think through your business model can help you build your "steering wheel" faster. Right now, jot down three people you could talk to about the business model for achieving your big idea.

Planning for the Journey

If your business model is your car's steering wheel, the next step is figuring out where to drive. Implementing a new strategy is like taking a road trip. Before setting out, you need to think through the best route and pack a few things. Once you're on the road, you need to continue managing the risks: anticipate traffic jams, check the gas gauge, and maybe check the tires after an especially rough road.

In everyday life, you do lots of things to proactively de-risk a journey to avoid frustration and ensure you aren't wasting time, energy, or money.

Applying the Re-Think How principle means doing the same type of proactive planning for your strategy—but from TWO perspectives:

- Your own understanding of how to execute

- The view of the people you need to take action and join you on the journey.

The Decision Makers' Journey

When you ask people to take *any* action, you are asking them to make a decision. The more significant the action, the bigger the decision.

Think about the last time you made a big decision. Did you think about it for a while? Research it? Weigh alternatives? Even for a small purchase online, it's easy to get lost in the decision-making process.

When people consider whether or not to change what they are doing and *take action with you*, there are emotions involved in the decision process that can slow things down.

There are four stages every one of us goes through when we make a decision: the Aware Stage, the Consider Stage, the Choose Stage, and the Benefit Stage. You can think of it as a continuing loop, where each stage leads into the other.

How fast people move through the stages of this Decision Makers' Journey is critical to your strategy's success. Anticipating what decision makers need in order to say, "Yes!" and taking the next step at each stage will directly speed up your results.

We're going to explore each stage of the Decision Makers' Journey. As we do, see if you relate to the challenges as a decision maker yourself. Then think about it from the perspective of those you want to join you.

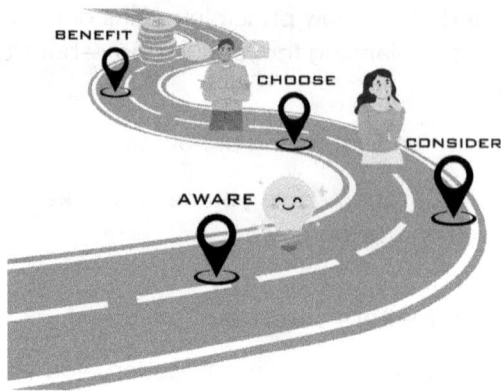

The Decision Makers' Journey

Decision Makers' Journey: The Aware Stage

Before making a decision about something, we have to realize there's a decision to make! In this Aware Stage, decision makers go through four phases of understanding.

If you applied these phases to a situation with your family car, it might look like this:

1. Unaware: What's the current condition? *(How's the car running?)*

2. Symptom Aware: Is something not working right? *(Was that a bump in the road, or was it the car making a strange noise?)*

3. Problem Aware: What is the underlying problem? *(Is this a problem with the steering or suspension or just the tire?)*

4. Solution Aware: What is the solution to this problem? *(Is it wiser to get this repaired or consider getting a new car?)*

At the Aware Stage, decision makers want to be *informed* and *educated* to understand what they are dealing with. They may not even be aware yet that there is a problem that needs solving! They might search online, see something about it in a magazine, hear about it on a podcast, or hear about it from someone close to them.

At this stage, decision makers know that they don't know enough, and you can help them by providing relevant information and new insights.

Decision Makers' Journey: The Consider Stage

Once a decision maker is aware there's a problem, there are more decisions to be made. A decision maker typically considers three options:

1. Solve it themselves.

2. Get help.

3. Do nothing.

Decision makers wrestle with questions in the Consider Stage, such as the following:

- What skills are required? *(Could I learn to fix a car?)*

- How much time will this take to fix? *(Do I have time to fix this myself?)*

- What about the quality and cost? *(Can someone else do this better and cheaper than I can?)*

- Can't I just wait and do nothing? *(Can I live with those weird sounds when I drive?)*

At this stage, decision makers welcome support and an objective guide to help them evaluate the problem from every angle. But in today's world, decision makers spend most of their time in the Consider Stage researching online. They may never even call you for support at all!

How can you be the "guide by the side" for your decision makers during the Consider Stage? By providing relevant information to help them through your website, blogs, newsletters, and educational forums. Everywhere you show up, make it clear that you understand the bigger questions they are wrestling with so you can provide value and build trust.

Decision Makers' Journey: The Choose Stage

Once your decision makers decide to get help to solve their problem, it's the moment of truth! A myriad of questions starts running through their heads:

- What criteria should I use to choose one solution over another? *(There are five mechanics in my area. How do I choose?)*

- Which solution is most cost-effective? *(If I go for the cheapest mechanic, will my car break down again faster?)*

- Has anyone else done this? *(What do the reviews say?)*

- How can I be sure I make the right decision? *(Will I regret this later?)*

With all the questions, drama, and tension, decision making at the Choose Stage can often slow down or get derailed completely.

You can help your decision makers move forward by anticipating their concerns and providing them with objective information about their options and risks. By serving as a trusted advisor during the Aware Stage and Consider Stage, you will have built credibility and a strong foundation to help them make the right decision at the Choose Stage.

Decision Makers' Journey: The Benefit Stage

We've come to a critical juncture in the Decision Makers' Journey: *the Benefit Stage is when you deliver on your promise.* This is where you have the opportunity to build trusting relationships, establish strong engagement and loyalty, and lay the foundation for your new strategy to sustain over time.

Early on in the Benefit Stage, your decision makers may ask themselves the following:

- Is this what I expected? *(Did this really fix the problem I came in for?)*

- Did I make a good decision? *(Was the cost of this repair really worth it?)*

- Does this organization listen to me? *(Did that customer survey mean anything?)*

And over time, your decision makers might ask the following:

- Is this problem still important to me? *(Do I really want to keep repairing this old car?)*

- Should I stay or leave? *(Should I continue using this repair shop?)*

During the Benefit Stage, your job is to ensure decision makers are confident their decision to take action was a good one. That means ensuring that you deliver on your commitments and engage with them so they feel valued. As you engage, listen for how their needs and priorities may be changing so you can remain relevant.

The Benefit Stage leads directly back to the next round of the Decision Makers' Journey, when people make another decision to stay or go. As they work with you, people decide whether they are willing to take action again. Only "actively" loyal decision makers will stay engaged for the long term and recommend others join in. Don't underestimate the need to continually support, educate, and listen.

Getting Inside Your Decision Makers' Minds

You never really understand a person until you consider things from his point of view . . . until you climb into his skin and walk around in it.

Harper Lee, novelist and author of *To Kill a Mockingbird*

How can you know what your decision makers are thinking? If you have access to the people you want to serve, go ask them! Arrange to sit down for a cup of coffee, talk to them on the street, or hold informal focus groups and surveys.

But what if you don't have easy access to your decision makers? Thankfully, online search and AI tools make doing this easier than ever before. I've included simple searches you can do in the "Get to Know Your Decision Makers" exercise.

Just an hour of this kind of online research can spark new insights and provide a solid basis for further interviews and testing. When you take the time to "get inside their minds," you can plan a smoother journey for your decision makers and enable them to say, "Yes!" faster.

GET TO KNOW YOUR DECISION MAKERS

Using search/AI tools, you can explore your decision makers' mindset with queries like the examples below. Download this exercise at bonus.fasttrackyourbigidea.com.

Search Like a Worried Decision Maker

Start by walking in the shoes of your target decision makers. What kinds of answers might they be searching for in the middle of the night? *Type into your favorite search engine the actual words they might use.* For instance,

- "How do I achieve *(the goals of this decision maker)*?"

- "What is the best way to solve *(the topic/problem you solve)*?"

- "What are the top 10 mistakes I should avoid when it comes to *(the topic/problem you solve)*?"

Review the results, looking for the type of language used and questions that follow. Understand how others are guiding your target decision makers. Do you agree? Do you have new insights you can contribute?

Explore Concerns at Each Stage of the Decision Makers' Journey

Use AI to gain insights into your decision makers' mindset at each different stage of their journey with this kind of prompt:

"We are talking to *(titles/attributes of your target decision makers)*. List the questions they will have at each stage of their decision-making journey (Aware, Consider, Choose, Benefit) as they think about *(the topic/problem you solve)*. At each stage, what emotions, concerns, and priorities might they have?"

Eavesdrop on Conversations with Your Target Decision Makers

Look for videos and podcast interviews with people who represent your target decision makers. Use this query:

"List five recent interviews with *(title of your target decision makers)* about *(the topic/problem you solve)*." As these decision makers speak about real-world concerns, pull up a chair and listen for their language and in what stage of the Decision Makers' Journey they might be.

Walking the Decision Makers' Journey

Experiencing your Decision Makers' Journey can be fun and enlightening—and *humbling*! You will gain insights about your target decision makers, and you will see gaps that you haven't addressed.

When I run Decision Makers' Journey programs with my clients, we start by auditing the current journey. Then we drill into areas where their decision makers may be getting stuck. In conversations after the workshops, participants often share ah-ha's like these:

"We have an innovative solution, but most of our prospects don't even realize they have a problem. We've completely missed the Aware Stage! No wonder we're struggling to get leads!"

—CEO of a startup

"If people don't see the problem we solve as urgent, they won't donate. We've just assumed people are concerned about our cause, so we focused on why we're the best at solving it. I realized from this exercise that unless we help people understand the bigger consequences of our cause in the Aware and Consider stages, it doesn't matter that we're better!"

—Executive Director of a nonprofit

"This workshop was an eye-opener. I always thought my job was done once we sold our offering. I never considered how crucial it is to stay engaged in the Benefit Stage. If budgets get tight or key users leave or support is frustrating, our customers could easily cancel!"

—Product Manager of a services company

Keep your decision makers front and center as you plan your new strategy. When you have a choice, choose the path that makes it easier for them to say, "Yes!" at each step. They'll appreciate it, and you'll get results faster.

For ideas to leverage the Decision Makers' Journey with your team, go to bonus.fasttrackyourbigidea.com.

DE-RISK SYSTEM FOR IMPACT®
PRINCIPLE 5

ANTICIPATE WHAT IF: PLANNING FOR POTHOLES AND POSSIBILITIES

One common mistake leaders make when they embark on a new strategy is to put all the focus on their launch, the "big reveal" of their exciting new idea. But most of your impact happens down the road, in the day-to-day interactions with your decision makers as you implement your new strategy. What will the road along your journey look like?

This?   Or this?

Over time, despite all your planning, potholes will inevitably show up along the road. You may risk disappointing those you serve or incur unexpected costs as you address last-minute surprises. You may risk exhausting your team, damaging your reputation, or missing out on opportunities for growth because you're up to your elbows fixing potholes. This is also where you, as a leader, may start to lose confidence.

In an uncertain world, risk is a constant. Road conditions will change. The assumptions you make up front, even ones that prove true early on, may evolve into dangerous biases that blind you. Monitoring your risk on a regular basis and looking ahead for what is coming is simply good "de-risk discipline."

> *In an uncertain world, risk is a constant.*

How can you best manage risk down the road? By doing some regular WHAT IF Thinking.

Buckle Your Seat Belt: Things Might Get Bumpy

In case of sudden turbulence, buckle
your seat belts low and tight on your lap . . .
Airline Flight Attendant Safety Speech

Can you recite the standard safety speech that airline flight attendants all over the world recite before takeoff? "Sudden turbulence" can result in confusion, disorder, and maybe even conflict. The underlying message from the flight crew is this: *things might get a little bumpy—but we're going to be ready!*

As a leader driving your organization in a new direction, what kind of seat belt do you have in place if things get a little bumpy?

Decision making becomes more complex in a turbulent organizational environment or changing marketplace. Our brains are wired to protect us, and when we see risk—even if it isn't physical danger—our brain sends us signals that create a fight-or-flight reaction. However, if you have considered scenarios about what you might do in that type of situation, the turbulence can feel a lot less scary.

WHAT IF Thinking with your organization can help you lead through turbulence. By helping your team consider different scenarios in the future, you are all more prepared for whatever comes up. This leverages what our brains are uniquely wired to do.

Neuroscientist Angus Fletcher, a professor at Ohio State University's Project Narrative, the leading think tank for story science, describes the brain's capacity to create WHAT IF scenarios as "storythinking." In his book *Storythinking: The New Science of Narrative Intelligence*, Fletcher highlights that the brain is a "huge improviser of possible plots, plans, and stories."[20]

When we don't have a plan, our brain starts to feel fear. Regular WHAT IF Thinking can help train our brains to create imaginative ways to solve problems, big and small. Fletcher's research shows that by regularly creating stories about

WHAT IF, we can dramatically increase curiosity, empathy, creativity, confidence, and resilience. The result is that risk seems more manageable.

Putting WHAT IF Thinking into Practice

My friend Bharat Dave is a former corporate executive and serial entrepreneur who now mentors CEOs of start-ups. When it comes to managing risk, he guides, "If you're going to spend *two days* to plan your entire year, spend at least *two hours* talking about your risks and how you'd handle them. It can actually give you and your team new energy you didn't think you had."

But how? A structured "WHAT IF Thinking" Session can ensure you capture meaningful insights and actions. WHAT IF Thinking in a group of people with diverse perspectives provides the greatest value.

I've provided a "WHAT IF Thinking" Session guide to start the ball rolling. Make sure you explore both the downside risk and also the risk of missing big opportunities.

End with hope: Identify what you can do today to prepare for what might be coming down the road. For instance, you might diversify your suppliers in case one supplier goes bankrupt, cross-train employees, or set up partnerships to ensure you have the capacity to handle big spikes in demand.

Or you may simply need to go do research about risks you hadn't considered before. By identifying steps you can take *now*, you and your team will feel more confident about handling uncertainties down the road.

A "What If THINKING" SESSION

This exercise is designed to help teams come up with imaginative ways to solve problems and manage risk. Download a copy at bonus.fasttrackyourbigidea.com.

Step 1: *Establish a Common Understanding of Our Strategy*

Ask: What is our understanding of Why (the problem we are solving) and Why You (why our organization is unique)?

Discuss: Share and come up with a common view. (If there's a lot of disagreement, resolve that first.)

Step 2: *Explore What Ifs*

Ask: Jot down risks to our achieving our strategy (external or internal):

- What windows of opportunity do we not want to miss?
- What are we depending on that might be negatively disrupted?

Discuss: Share and identify common themes.

Step 3: *Explore Our Assumptions*

Ask: What do we believe is true that causes us to see these as risks?

Discuss: How do we know these assumptions are true? How do we find out?

Step 4: *Explore What We Can Do Today*

Ask: Write down two things our organization could do to get ready for any of the risks discussed. (They don't have to be the risks you brought up.)

Discuss: Share all ideas. Vote on which ones are most actionable. Discuss who would need to be involved and identify someone (in the session) to take the lead in exploring how to execute.

Getting Comfortable Talking About Risk: Pre-Mortems

What if people don't *want* to talk about risk?

My friend Howard Fields thrives on tech innovation. He has tackled countless projects that leveraged technology to revolutionize organizations. What irks him most? The post-mortems. Teams often confess they sensed trouble early but stayed silent, muttering vague excuses like, "I just didn't feel comfortable bringing it up," "I thought everybody else saw it too," or "I thought my view didn't matter." Known risks hang unspoken in the air, often leading to major fallout. Silence isn't always golden; it can be costly.

So how do *you* foster a space where people can confess their concerns? Well, consider this: why do people pay good money to watch disaster movies? Whether you're watching *The Towering Inferno* or *Titanic*, seeing things go terribly wrong can be fun, as long as you are in your seat safely eating popcorn. The same thing can be true as you and your team envision how your new strategy will play out.

Instead of a post-mortem, consider holding a "pre-mortem." It's sort of a WHAT IF Thinking Exercise: *Disaster Version*. The idea is to imagine you are looking into an unbelievably accurate crystal ball. You envision your strategy playing out like a movie but—*yikes!* Suddenly disaster hits! (Make it fun. Disasters can range from practical to outrageous, from supplier issues to alien invasions.)

Then you stop the action and ask everyone to jot down the reason why that disaster happened. Somehow, people can suddenly see new vulnerabilities in your plan. As everyone shares their observations, note any themes that emerge.

After you've wallowed in the disaster for a while, you can start to identify the underlying drivers. What would early warning signs look like if you started heading in the wrong direction? What can you do today to avoid them?

Every aspect of your new strategy will not go perfectly. But by doing a pre-mortem, you can start taking action now to avoid some possible disasters down the road.

For a team that is overwhelmed with all there is to do, pre-mortems can create new energy. When you and your team identify critical issues that could have caused your strategy to fail, and figure out how to avoid them, you all suddenly become the heroes of your movie! Revel in the victory—and pass the popcorn!

You can download information about the Pre-Mortem Method at bonus.fasttrackyourbigidea.com.

Establish a Regular WHAT IF Rhythm

Regularly anticipating WHAT IF scenarios can help you and your team prepare for the potholes and possibilities you may encounter as you execute your strategy. De-risking your strategy this way enlists everyone to anticipate and contribute to solutions before they are needed. It also builds team confidence that you're ready for anything.

DE-RISK SYSTEM FOR IMPACT®
PRINCIPLE 6

OPTIMIZE TO LEAD:
NAVIGATING RISK OVER TIME

De-risking your strategy will help you avoid common mistakes and speed your journey. But optimizing risk isn't a one-time event; it's a way of life. Stewarding risk requires open, ongoing communication. This chapter will discuss ways to build a strong culture where living with risk is more comfortable and people can thrive, even in the middle of uncertainty.

> *Optimizing risk isn't a one-time event; it's a way of life.*

Cultivate a Risk-Savvy Culture

Leaders who understand the principles of the DE-RISK SYSTEM FOR IMPACT® will want to incorporate them into daily conversations. As your team becomes more comfortable discussing risk, they will also become more confident about bringing up new opportunities, taking action to avert problems, and adapting as new situations arise.

As you go through the de-risking process, capture the risks and assumptions at each step. Then set up time on a regular basis to step back and evaluate how well you are managing the risks you identified earlier, whether they are still relevant, and whether new risks are on the horizon. Consider which of your assumptions are proving true, which are not turning out as planned, and where you need to adapt.

Make sure you are talking about your biggest assumptions and risks as part of your regular strategy progress reviews and place the topic *first* on the agenda. This will provide both clarity and context for more informed decision making.

Develop a Rhythm for Sensing Change

WHAT IF Thinking can help you become more open about seeing changes around you. You actively start looking for data that makes you uncomfortable rather than ignoring it.

During one make-or-break launch I worked on, the general manager was worried. She was pouring a lot of money into a new innovative offering but was concerned about our timing. "Are we trying to be too innovative? Will our customers understand it? But on the other hand, what if we wait and the competition gets there first?"

So this courageous general manager tasked the entire team with listening and sensing for what made everyone *uncomfortable*. The team would regularly compare notes on how fast the market was unfolding. "Do customers seem willing to allocate funding to solve this problem?" "Is the competition talking about this problem the same way we are?" "Are suppliers investing in inventories?"

It was tense, but looking at the market with open eyes made the WHAT IFS more concrete. In the end, the team narrowed the initial offering and go-to-market efforts to a niche where traction was most likely. The result was faster revenue, higher customer satisfaction, and earlier profits.

Whether you are sensing changes through informal conversations, formal surveys, pulse reports from the front line, or listening tours with customers, partners, suppliers, and funders, make sure you and your team are keeping your eyes and ears open.

Then get your team together to hold regular "sensing reviews." These reviews are opportunities to share knowledge, identify patterns in customer demand and behavior, evaluate what competitors are doing differently, and understand trends and issues that are becoming relevant to your strategy.

Lead by Example

Leading a new strategy requires that your organization continually adapt to a changing environment. But sometimes it's not the strategy that needs changing—it's the *leader*!

The same visionary leader who inspires people to launch a big idea can become a detriment as the strategy unfolds. Sometimes, visionary leaders can get so invested in their plan that they become resistant to feedback and market trends, rigid in making decisions, or unwilling to develop new skills.

The very attributes that make leaders successful at launching new strategies (vision, ownership for results, attention to getting things right) can lead to bottlenecks, slow decision making, and under-leveraging team members' skills and expertise. The result is that people get frustrated and leave, and the strategy falters.

Sometimes it's not the strategy that needs changing—it's the leader!

"Founder syndrome" refers to a phenomenon whereby founders, or other long-standing leaders of organizations, struggle to adapt as their organization grows and evolves. Many visionaries, from inventor Henry Ford to aircraft maker Howard Hughes to Apple's Steve Jobs, have found it difficult to relinquish control, delegate to others, and adapt their style. In some cases, boards of directors have had to step in and replace leaders who weren't willing to adapt, with lots of drama and disruptions along the way.

In his landmark strategic planning book *Grow or Die: The Unifying Principles of Transformation*, George Ainsworth-Land challenges us to realize that everything needs to grow, or it will eventually wither and become irrelevant—from plants to countries, from companies to people.

If you are serious about making your strategy succeed and grow, you will need to be just as intentional about continuing to grow personally as a leader. Reflect on how you will need to improve *your* skills to lead more effectively as your organization grows. Working on your own personal growth will not only make this journey more successful—it will be more fun!

Confidently Address Risk

Every new strategy has risks. But when you are intentional about addressing risk from the start, you improve the likelihood you will succeed. We have now walked through all six principles of the DE-RISK SYSTEM FOR IMPACT®:

- RECONFIRM WHY AND WHY NOW

- VALIDATE WHY YOU

- CLARIFY WHO

- RE-THINK HOW

- ANTICIPATE WHAT IF

- OPTIMIZE TO LEAD

As you implement your new strategy, these principles can help you confidently address the risk and stay on course. The questions are: How are *you* de-risking your big idea today? Are these principles part of how you work? Where do you need to change the most?

Take a moment to identify the areas where de-risking can have the most impact for you in light of your stage. This ACCELERATION ADVANTAGE™ will provide clarity and build confidence in your strategy as you take the next step: ensuring people are aligned and ready to move forward with you.

Section 3 Key Takeaways
Get in Gear: De-Risking Your
Strategy for Impact

Risk is constant in an uncertain world. The DE-RISK SYSTEM FOR IMPACT® principles can help you manage risk more effectively and lead more confidently.

- When you clearly define WHY (the problem you solve), you will be able to navigate uncertainty more easily. This will also attract people to help. Confirming WHY NOW creates an urgency that moves people forward faster.

- VALIDATE WHY YOU to ensure you stand out as unique. Funders are faster to invest in your big idea when they understand what makes you and your approach unique.

- CLARIFY WHO needs to take action for your strategy to be successful. Even the best strategy will fail if people are confused, skeptical, or unaligned.

- RE-THINK HOW to sustain your strategy with a balanced business model and a Decision Makers' Journey that makes it easy for people to say, "Yes!" at every stage.

- WHAT IF Thinking can help train our brains to create imaginative ways to solve problems. When people can talk openly about risk, it reduces anxiety and risk becomes manageable.

- Sustaining your strategy requires that you OPTIMIZE TO LEAD. Regular risk and sensing reviews help you see a changing environment more clearly. You also need to be committed to growing personally as a leader.

Section 3 Notes and Action Steps
Get in Gear: De-Risking Your Strategy for Impact

(Jot down two to three things that jumped out that you can quickly apply.)

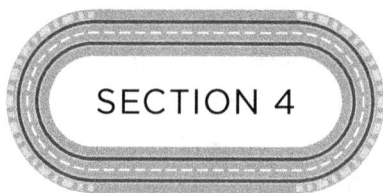

OVERDRIVE: ALIGNING FOR MAXIMUM TRACTION

*Building a visionary organization requires
one percent vision and 99 percent alignment.*
Jim Collins and Jerry Porras, researchers and authors of
Built to Last: Successful Habits of Visionary Companies

The concept of alignment seems pretty straightforward. When we get tires or train tracks or teeth aligned, things go more smoothly. You might be thinking, Isn't alignment simply the task of lining things up and going in the same direction? Well, not if you have to work with people. Aligning people is more nuanced. It requires that you bring people together, in agreement or alliance, so that they are able to support each other to accomplish an outcome.

Alignment is not something you do to people. Getting people aligned requires working *with* people, and that gets more complicated. When people aren't aligned, there can be serious consequences:

- *In personal relationships*, a lack of alignment results in disappointment and conflict. When friends, spouses, families, neighbors, or co-workers aren't aligned, they can get into huge fights or work at cross-purposes— which leads to huge fights!

- *Teams and organizations* that aren't aligned get frustrated, waste energy, and miss commitments. Whether they are playing soccer or developing software, teams that aren't in agreement won't achieve their potential. People get confused, decision making slows down, implementation is delayed, resources are wasted, and windows of opportunity are missed.

- *Ecosystems* comprised of many organizations working together have the potential to deliver significant value. Yet only 50 percent of companies report success in achieving more value when they work as part of an ecosystem.[21]

How well people are aligned will determine the success of your strategy. How you invite people to join you can make all the difference.

CHAPTER 12

GET ON BOARD OR ON ONE PAGE?

Years ago, I was sitting in a product launch status meeting with people from every function around the table. Our product was behind schedule, and everyone was on edge.

My role was to bring the product to market, and I knew we had a problem. The product wasn't working as we had promised. Our customer-facing teams would be confused, and our customers would be frustrated, which could negatively impact our ability to achieve revenue commitments.

So I asked, "What would it take to fix this problem before we launch? I recognize this might cause a delay, but if everything works correctly from the start, it will help us achieve our revenue goals faster."

The head of product development swiftly responded, "The train has left the station. Either get on board or get out of the way." All conversation stopped, and the unanswered concerns just hung in the air.

Technically, we were all aligned—like train cars, we were all following behind the conductor, like it or not. But that didn't mean we all believed we were heading toward the right destination!

A leader's call to "get on board," as in this scenario, can often be perceived negatively. The idiom, rooted in the 15th century, initially referred to seafaring vessels and then later to trains. The captain or conductor would call out, "All aboard!" and passengers would scurry to get on the ship or train to a *predetermined destination* along a *predetermined route*.

The underlying message people hear when they are called to "get on board" is often "Look, I've laid out this perfect strategy. I have all the answers. Just do this my way—no questions asked."

Instead of asking people to "get on board," what if you invited them to *get on the same page* with you?

When your team takes on a new strategy, you are much like a group of mountain climbers aiming to conquer Mt. Everest. Like mountain climbers, your team members and partners come together with different backgrounds and experiences. But mountain climbers always start by *getting on the same page*!

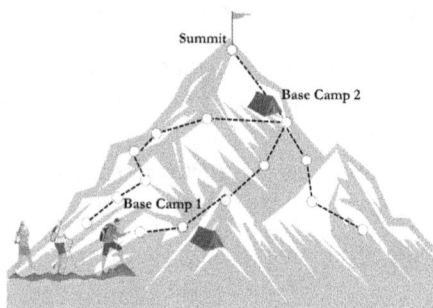

*Get On the Same Page to
Drive Your Strategy*

When the stakes are high and lives are on the line, there is no room for ambiguity. A successful climbing team agrees to a common game plan to reach the summit. Together, they analyze a topographic map of the mountain to study the terrain, weigh various routes, and discuss how they will handle challenges. Getting on the same page takes work, but they know it is critical if they are to reach the top and return safely.

Getting everyone on the same page to drive your strategy will take work too, but it will be easier when you have a game plan.

CHAPTER 13

YOUR
ACCELERATION ADVANTAGE™:
A GAME PLAN FOR ALIGNMENT

No amount of team building, "trust falls," and singing "Kumbaya" will ensure people are on the same page and ready to move forward. One of the factors required to create an ACCELERATION ADVANTAGE™ is making sure you have a plan to *align* people.

You can create a solid Game Plan for Alignment by applying these principles right from the start:

- Principle #1: Precisely define your destination.

- Principle #2: Listen early to diverse perspectives.

- Principle #3: Make clear who needs to do what.

- Principle #4: Continually recalibrate.

Let's dive into each of these principles and how they can help.

The ACCELERATION ADVANTAGE™
Go to Market Impact LLC

ALIGNMENT PRINCIPLE #1

Precisely Define Your Destination

The airport was swamped with people in bad moods due to weather-related flight delays, but one couple stood out. From their starry-eyed smiles and the bouquet the woman was carrying, I surmised they were heading off on their honeymoon. But as we started to board, I heard a commotion. It was the newlyweds having a meltdown. "What? San Jose, *California*? But we're going to San Jose, *Costa Rica*! And our flight is supposed to be taking off right now!" Confusion, panic, tears.

The lesson? Sometimes, when you think you're on the same page with others about where you're going, you're not. Getting really specific about your destination is crucial if you want to get results faster.

While a compelling Why can attract and inspire people to take a new direction, getting people aligned to actually *implement together* requires being much more specific. It requires you to define your *strategic destination.*

Your strategic destination needs to be tangible and measurable. Your timeline to accomplish it should be within twelve to eighteen months, or even within three years—but it has got to be near enough that people feel a sense of urgency to make it a reality. The clock is ticking.

Even with a strategic destination defined, leaders of new strategies often make the mistake of launching their big idea without clearly understanding the effort required. Have you ever seen this story play out?

> *Big Boss returns from a conference, fired up about a Big Idea to revolutionize the current situation. It will require a complete shift in direction, prompting a flurry of drop-everything-to-attend strategy meetings dubbed "Project Big Idea." However, everyone's workload is already overflowing. Realization sets in that*

regular work responsibilities now have to be accomplished after hours, dampening morale. As these meetings drag on, frustration mounts and skepticism grows. Big Boss, perplexed and frustrated that the leaders fail to grasp the wonderful Big Idea, is heard muttering, "I guess they just aren't as strategic as I thought."

Even when people are excited about your big idea, it's easy for them to get discouraged when they realize it is going to require more work than they can handle. To make sure everyone is clear on priorities and willing to execute together, it helps to look at two dimensions before you commit to a big undertaking:

- The degree of *impact* you can have on the problem you're trying to solve
- The amount of *effort* it will take to implement.

To assess these two dimensions, I find the Impact/Effort Matrix framework is helpful. It has roots in project management processes, drawn from the world of Six Sigma. It is often used when evaluating options for quality improvement and product development. The Impact/Effort Matrix is sometimes called the "Eisenhower Method" after American President Dwight Eisenhower, who was famous for using this matrix to make big decisions.

To use the Impact/Effort Matrix, have your team plot all options in the quadrants and focus on initiatives with high impact and low effort. This discussion helps educate cross-functional teams about what it will take to pull off an initiative. Starting with smaller, achievable successes builds credibility and momentum without exhausting the people you need to help you. Download the matrix at bonus.fasttrackyourbigidea.com.

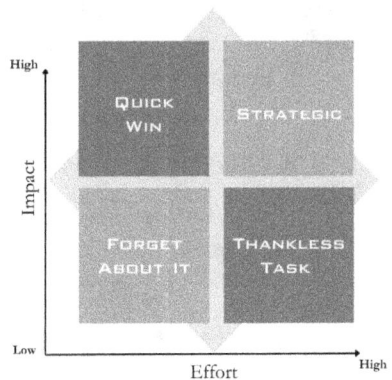

The Impact/Effort Matrix Based on Six Sigma Quality Processes[22]

ALIGNMENT PRINCIPLE #2
TAKE TIME TO LISTEN TO DIVERSE PERSPECTIVES

You've spent all day as a team, working through your strategy. The room is covered in flipcharts and colorful sticky notes. You look around and ask, "Does anyone have any concerns before we present this to the board tomorrow?"

Silence.

Great, right? Well, *maybe*.

Children learn on the playground that being different is risky. When it comes to bringing up contrary views, people take cues about what is acceptable (and unacceptable) based on those around them.

To Align or to Conform?

In his famous "Line Experiment," psychologist Solomon Asch asked college students to participate in a simple visual test to judge which line best matched another.[23] Only one person in the group was actually the test subject. Asch wanted to see how the test subjects would react after hearing the answers of other participants, who were all actors in the experiment.

The findings of Asch's experiment were telling:

- When all the actors answered this simple question *correctly*, the test subject got the answer right over 99% of the time.

- But when *every* actor responded *with the same incorrect* answer, more than one-third of the test subjects went along with the group—*even when they knew the other participants were wrong!*

- *If at least ONE actor responded with the correct answer*, less than 5% of the test participants went along with the group.

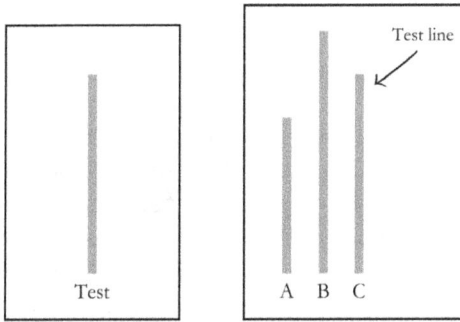

Asch Line Experiment
Based on research by Solomon Asch[24]

Asch concluded that people tend to conform when they feel peer pressure to go along with the majority. When their view is different from others, they may doubt their own accuracy.

Getting aligned is *not* about forcing people to conform because they feel pressure. In fact, that's the last thing you want. Remember that story about the product launch where I was told to get on board because "the train had left the station"? I ended up conforming when no one else spoke up. I was intimidated. Unfortunately, our organization paid the consequences. We missed dates, frustrated the sales force, disappointed customers, and missed our revenue objectives.

If I had fully understood the power of diverse perspectives at the time, I could have been bolder! But we hadn't created a culture or system to allow people in that room to speak honestly about risk.

> *Getting aligned is not about forcing people to conform.*

Getting people to understand and agree with each other takes time. People need to express their perspectives and concerns and process new information. And sometimes you'll be the one learning and adjusting.

When people have the time to understand and think through a new direction, ask questions, and offer their own ideas and improvements, they are more likely to join you for the long run. As a bonus, you'll be more confident that your path is the right one.

Just be prepared for some spirited debate along the way.

The Value of Spirited Debate

I once had a boss who both inspired and frustrated me. He had a great vision and deftly steered our organization's transformation strategy. But he seemed inconsistent when it came to providing direction. At times, he'd give detailed guidance about how to address what seemed like a minor issue. Other times, he'd sit quietly while our leadership team held endless debates.

One day, after he explained how to fix a quirky spreadsheet issue, I confronted my boss's inconsistency. "Why are you giving me such a detailed answer for such a small problem, yet you let our leadership team flounder for *hours* in fruitless debates over much bigger issues about our company's turnaround? You've obviously thought a lot about this already. Why don't you just make these decisions yourself?"

He sat back and smiled. "Welcome to spirited debate. Every person on this leadership team needs to understand the assumptions we're making, the trade-offs we have to deal with, and the risks we're taking. You all need to decide together where we are taking this organization—or our turnaround will fail."

From that day forward, I stopped seeing our team's spirited debate as fruitless or frustrating. I appreciated that it had a purpose: to ensure we were all invested in our new direction.

How invested are people in *your* strategy?

Employees often ask for "the answer from the top." But even when they get an answer, they continue to second-guess the direction, especially if the new strategy requires people to grapple with hard choices. Trade-offs are not comfortable.

When employees, partners, and customers can provide input to shape an organization's direction, they believe in it more. They feel more ownership. Why is that?

People will feel more invested in your strategy if they help build it. Research by McKinsey Consulting shows that the best-performing companies encourage rigorous discussion of new initiatives: "Colleagues in these companies challenge one another, listen to minority views, and scrutinize assumptions. Particularly in 'big bet' scenarios, the most significant predictor of successful decision making is the quality of the discussions and debate."[25]

People will feel more invested in your strategy if they help build it.

Inviting people to help you shape answers to challenging questions means they'll provide new perspectives, wrestle alongside you with the trade-offs, and understand the consequences of the ultimate decision. It will also build *trust*.

As you initiate these conversations, be quick to listen and slow to weigh in with your answers. Your team's diverse perspectives can make your strategy stronger. When you're done, it will no longer be "your strategy" but "ours," enabling everyone to shape something new together.

Ensuring Different Perspectives: The Walt Disney Method

When the stakes are high, it's easy for people to get locked into their points of view. Leadership teams and boards can easily get stuck. Fortunately, filmmaker Walt Disney had this figured out. Walt was famous for looking at an idea for a film from three different angles at the same time. He would:

- Start by focusing on the vision, imagining the whole story with all its possibilities in living color.

- Get realistic, considering the practical implications of producing the film.

- Put himself in a front-row seat, thinking through how the audience might experience and critique the film.

Walt's approach inspired neuro-linguistic programming expert Robert Dilts to frame a methodology for parallel thinking. The "Walt Disney Method" can improve team collaboration and give dreamers, realists, and critics alike a little elbow room. I've provided an exercise you can use with your team.

As the group "wears" each character, all points of view are considered. People who normally lean toward one perspective will get a good workout by stretching outside their comfort zones and seeing things from a new angle. Fears, worries, or objections that might otherwise have lingered in people's minds get openly discussed and enable your team to co-create possibilities.

Next time you're tempted to silence the dreamers, the realists, or the critics on your team, consider what you might be missing if their voices aren't heard. Who knows what "wonderful world" you may be able to create together!

THE WALT DISNEY METHOD EXERCISE

This exercise is designed to ensure all perspectives are heard when considering a new strategy or getting one back on track. Download a copy at bonus.fasttrackyourbigidea.com.

Welcome to the Show

Discuss the purpose of the exercise and the mindset of each of these characters.

Character #1 *The Dreamer* asks, "Why?"

As a group, put on the dreamer's mindset and discuss the problem our strategy needs to solve and capture the possibilities to create impact.

Character #2 *The Realist* dives into the practical implications.

As a group, put on the realist's mindset and discuss what it will take to make this strategy work? Capture key assumptions.

Character #3 *The Critic* steps back and identifies the critical success factors.

As a group, put on the critic's mindset and discuss the risks of our strategy, including the risk of missed opportunities.

Cast Party

Discuss the common themes and important issues. Share personal learnings.

Negotiate Alignment Faster: The Power of Acknowledgement

If you are urgent about getting results, you may find all this "listening for different perspectives" a little frustrating. When people go on and on about their different views, it can feel like the team is getting stuck.

Don't worry. You're actually making progress.

Before people can agree to a new strategy or take action to do something new, they need to understand how it aligns with their beliefs and values. They may ask questions about implications and consequences that seem far-fetched, but these questions are all part of their own internal alignment process.

For some, though, that's not enough. Many people are *unable* to embrace a new concept until their perspective is publicly *acknowledged*. Don't think of this step as obstruction. It's actually a necessary part of the alignment process to foster acceptance and progress.

CIA hostage negotiator Chris Voss knows this too well. In his book *Never Split the Difference: Negotiating as If Your Life Depended on It*, Voss says, "The two sweetest words in any negotiation are *'That's right.'*"[26] This is the point when a person confirms back to you that they believe you truly *understand* their perspective.

Want to move things forward when people go on and on with their point of view? Simply confirm you've *heard* them! Summarize their concerns by paraphrasing their own words. Acknowledge the consequences they are concerned about and the emotions they stir. In doing this, you powerfully show them you really *do* understand their point of view. You don't necessarily have to agree with them, but you have given them an even greater gift—*respect*.

This one step can be a game-changer when striving to align people to move forward. It can dissolve barriers, build connections, and allow people to transition to a new beginning, *even if they don't necessarily like it*!

ALIGNMENT PRINCIPLE #3

Make Clear Who Needs to Do What

A Formula 1 race is a fast and furious journey of 190 miles around a track. When drivers pull in for a pit stop, fractions of a second can make all the difference whether they can even stay in the race, much less win. More than twenty people jump in to take action together: stabilize the car, change the tires, refuel, adjust the aerodynamics, and safely release the car to continue the journey. Everyone is crystal clear on their role, motivated, and qualified to execute a specific action.

Clarity is critical whether you are in a race or leading a strategic initiative. Yet leaders who get excited about their big ideas can make the mistake of using too many generalities. "We're transforming the market!" "You can help create a movement!" It all translates into a flurry of emotion, often without measurable results.

When you want to get results faster, it's essential to take the time to get very clear about WHO needs to take action from three perspectives:

1. Who can *accelerate* results?
2. Who is *motivated* to take action?
3. Who *owns* which action?

Let's explore each perspective.

Who Can Accelerate Results?

To accelerate your new strategy, focus your time and energy on the people most likely to take action. Start by identifying the *target markets, organizations,* and *audiences* with whom your strategy will resonate most.

Your Target Market is comprised of everyone working on the same problem you are—from *every* angle. This could include customers, suppliers, nonprofits, regulators, educators, researchers, or investors. The more narrowly you define your target market, the more efficient you can be in finding and partnering with other people who care about that specific problem. Say you have a new approach that will revolutionize the speed of healing wounds. Instead of targeting all healthcare organizations, you might target a narrower set of decision makers, like emergency room personnel and suppliers.

Your Target Organizations are the ones within your target market that need *exactly* what you offer—they just may not know you yet. Your offer is a perfect fit for what they need. (Even if you primarily serve consumers, you still may have organizations that serve those consumers whom you may want to work with.)

Your Target Audiences are individuals who can take action or encourage others. Your audience is comprised of ideal decision makers and influencers.

- *Ideal decision makers* are willing to invest their time, talent, and treasure to get things done. They will quickly understand the problem you solve and the solution you offer and want to take action with you. Clearly defining the attributes of your ideal decision makers can help you find them faster within an organization. They may have common demographics (age, role, title, geography) or common "psychographics" (attitudes, values, needs).

- *Influencers* are people who relate to the problem you solve but will not necessarily be implementing your strategy *themselves*. They'll help you accelerate results by lending their name and reputation to your cause. Influencers move people to action because of their authority, knowledge, position, relationship, or resources. They could be leaders of organizations, philanthropists, industry analysts, technical or government experts, or media reporters. (Note: the term "influencer" has taken on a whole new meaning in the age of social media. Make sure you identify which influencers your ideal decision makers actually respect and listen to. Hollywood stars may not be the influencers you need.)

With an intentional plan for outreach to your target market, target organizations, and target audiences, you can focus your energy on people with knowledge and influence around the problem you want to solve. But within the pool of all the people who *can* help, how do you find people who *will* help?

Who is Motivated to Take Action?

Getting things done is more fun when you're working with people who are motivated. And if those people also have influence, they'll be able to encourage *others* to join you too! Consider the following:

- *Motivation:* How informed or engaged is this organization/person/role in the problem you are striving to solve? Are they already aware of the problem and energized to tackle it? Are they currently uninformed about the specific problem? Or completely uninterested?

- *Influence:* How much can this organization/role/person encourage others to believe that your strategy is a good one? Even if they aren't going to do a lot of the heavy lifting themselves, could this person connect you with others who can help? Or could they *slow down* progress if they don't understand and believe in your new direction?

I find that the Motivation/Influence Matrix works well to visualize these two dimensions. It is based on a tool originally developed by Aubrey Mendelow to help project managers understand that stakeholders need to be dealt with differently. I frequently use this matrix to help boards, leadership teams, and community groups focus their time and effort when enlisting support or funding for their new strategy.

The exercise can help your team brainstorm different organizations, roles, and people and develop a plan to approach them best. Each quadrant requires a different approach: Inform, Engage, Enlist, or Ally. Focusing your energy first on the top right quadrant, "High Influence, High Motivation," can speed results.

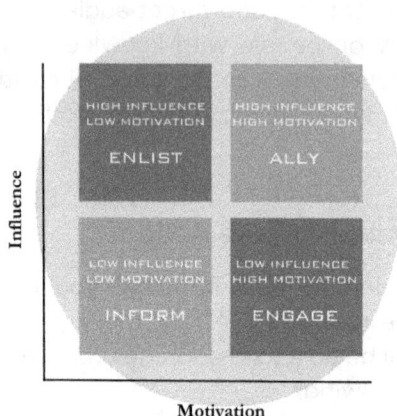

The Motivation/Influence Matrix
Based on work by Aubrey Mendelow[27]

Using the Motivation/Influence Matrix can help people get on one page and prioritize their efforts to move forward faster. For a copy, go to bonus.fasttrackyourbigidea.com.

Who Owns What Action?

Did you hear the story about the four partners in a startup who were having trouble getting funding? They were named Everybody, Somebody, Anybody, and Nobody.

> *There was an important job to be done, and Everybody was sure that Somebody would do it. Anybody could have done it, but Nobody did it. Somebody got angry about that because it was Everybody's job. Everybody thought Anybody could do it, but Nobody realized that Everybody wouldn't do it. It ended up that Everybody blamed Somebody when Nobody did what Anybody could have.[28]*

Okay, Charles Osgood's poem is a little hokey, but if you've ever led a new initiative, it may be uncomfortably familiar!

When the stakes are high for a new initiative, getting clarity about who owns what action is imperative.

The RACI Model to the Rescue

The "RACI" model can help you eliminate ambiguity about who owns what. The project management tool was conceived in the 1950s to address complex projects involving many different people and organizations. For each important task, simply decide who is:

- **R**esponsible: Who does the work to complete this task?

- **A**ccountable: Who is authorized to sign off that this task is complete? Who will deal with the consequences if you fall short of the goal?

- **C**onsulted: Who needs to provide input based on specific expertise or area of responsibility?

- **I**nformed: Who needs to be kept in the loop along the way because they have to work with the outcome after the task is completed?

For a template to clarify who does what using the RACI format, go to bonus.fasttrackyourbigidea.com.

Identifying the organizations and people who can accelerate results and are motivated to take action will help you focus your efforts. Ensuring everyone knows who owns which action and who can make decisions will help speed results.

But beware: this is not a one-time effort. You'll need to keep checking in with people to make sure everyone is on the same page.

ALIGNMENT PRINCIPLE #4
Continuously Recalibrate

A commercial airline is scheduled to go from New York to Paris. As the crew arrives, they quickly work to get aligned: review the flight plan, coordinate with air traffic control, clarify responsibilities, ensure the aircraft is ready, board the passengers, and depart. But it doesn't end there. Over the course of their eight-hour journey, the crew constantly scans and interprets new information about changes in weather, the aircraft, and the passengers. They continually adapt in order to safely reach their destination on time.

In the same way, when you're driving a new strategy, staying aligned as a team in the midst of change is part of the job. Even when leaders put together a detailed plan with well-aligned metrics, strategies can derail when the original assumptions change. Staying aligned requires recalibrating based on new information, and it starts with being willing to confront reality.

I've been surprised and frustrated by how often a leadership team or board will spend *hours* in meetings reviewing mind-numbing metrics that indicate they have a problem and yet avoid talking about the elephant-in-the-room issues that are causing it. The issues vary, but they are avoided because they are usually uncomfortable.

For instance:

- A disruptive market change or competitor is being ignored.

- A senior leader is avoiding making a difficult decision.

- New leaders have joined who don't agree with the original strategy.

- Confidence was damaged when the organization failed to deliver last time.

Alignment is fragile. It takes work, and some of that work means confronting uncomfortable truths. Expect to have to constantly recalibrate to stay aligned over time.

Two things must be in place to make recalibrating easier:

1. A cadence for sensing change and re-evaluating your strategy
2. A way to hold difficult conversations when things aren't working.

Sensing Change

In Section 3, we discussed de-risking by "sensing" changes in your environment. While this is important to do up front, it isn't a one-and-done effort.

When you're driving a new strategy, staying aligned as a team in the midst of change is part of the job.

As you implement your strategy, set aside regular time to consider the implications of changes in your environment. This can help your organization feel more comfortable and prepared. Boston Consulting Group calls this "signal advantage."[29] You're not just collecting tons of data points about what is changing around you; you're taking time as a team to evaluate the trends, challenge your assumptions, and make operational interventions.

Holding regular team sessions to recalibrate based on new input can help you not only get on the same page about today's situation but potentially adapt your business so you are better positioned for the future. The problem is, it's not just your environment that can change.

When People Change

> *Things do not change; we change.*
> Henry David Thoreau, poet and philosopher

> *People change and forget to tell each other.*
> Lillian Hellman, playwright

A relationship, team, organization, or partnership can come completely undone when one key person changes. There are many reasons why this can happen. It might be due to health issues, a personal or professional crisis, or changes in an individual's life priorities or interests. Or it might be that an individual is simply overwhelmed and drowning in fear.

If you notice that a key leader on your team has changed so much that they are no longer effective in their role, *do not ignore it*. Take the time for an open, honest conversation to understand the situation. This person may need support or training or to be moved to a more suitable role. Sometimes, you may need to part ways.

When you get the right people in the right positions, your organization will be able to adapt more easily. But as Jim Collins points out in his book *Good to Great: Why Some Companies Make the Leap . . . and Others Don't*, "If you have the wrong people, it doesn't matter whether you discover the right direction; you *still* won't have a great company."[30]

When things aren't working, it's imperative that you step up to the plate and have difficult conversations, or your strategy will falter.

Aligning People Requires Difficult Conversations

> *Finding good players is easy.*
> *Getting them to play as a team is another story.*
> Casey Stengel, professional baseball player and manager

In her book *Fierce Conversations: Achieving Success at Work and in Life, One Conversation at a Time*, Susan Scott challenges us to hold "fierce conversations" that are robust, intense, strong, powerful, passionate, eager, and unbridled. Fierce conversations allow us to come to terms with reality.

Whether launching big mergers or small projects, I have found Scott's "Mineral Rights Conversation Model" useful with individuals or teams who aren't on the same page. The name is based on the idea that when you drill for minerals in the ground, you need to go really deep to get to the most valuable stuff. Surface-level conversations don't yield meaningful answers.

Scott identified seven questions that help people "mine" for greater clarity, improve understanding, *and* lay the groundwork for change. These questions can be used to reflect on your own perspective and to guide a productive conversation with another person about why you aren't aligned.

(Heads up: Question #5 is the toughest. Asking "What is my own contribution to this problem?" takes soul-searching. Don't let anyone, including yourself, dodge that one!)

Is a cross-functional project team squabbling as a deadline looms? Is a member of your leadership team avoiding a difficult personnel decision? Is the CEO not stepping up? It's important to hold an open, honest, "fierce" conversation. It can be a first step for getting back into alignment.

As we've seen, you can lead people to align and achieve great things together only when you:

- Are clear on your destination
- Seek diverse perspectives
- Clarify who needs to take which action
- Recalibrate as you sense things changing.

Leveraging these principles as you build your Game Plan for Alignment can help your organization avoid common pitfalls—that is, unless you have an alignment problem of your own.

THE MINERAL RIGHTS CONVERSATION MODEL[31]

This model, from Susan Scott's book, Fierce Conversations: Achieving Success at Work and in Life, One Conversation at a Time, *can help you gain greater clarity, improve understanding, and lay the groundwork for change. Use it to prepare for a productive conversation when trying to figure out why you aren't aligned with another person.*

1. What is the most important thing we should be talking about today?

2. How long has this been going on?

3. What results is this producing? Who is this impacting? When you consider these results, what do you feel?

4. If nothing changes, what is likely to occur? When you imagine that scenario, what do you feel?

5. What has been your own contribution to this problem?

6. What would be your ideal outcome? If you succeed in this, what difference will that make?

7. What is the next most powerful step you can take? When will you take it? When can I follow up with you?

CHAPTER 14

THE MOST IMPORTANT ALIGNMENT: YOUR OWN

Some people are getting worried about Artificial Intelligence (AI) these days. There seems to be a big alignment problem brewing.

Brian Christian, author of *The Alignment Problem: Machine Learning and Human Values*, warns that unless AI is aligned with human values, machines will make their *own* decisions— and we may not like some of them![32] For instance:

- If you tell a self-driving car to go from point A to point B, it could run over a jaywalking pedestrian unless you train it to value people over speed.

- If you ask an AI chatbot to field customer service calls, you'll need to train it to value keeping customers. Otherwise, it could refuse to give returns to optimize profit or spew unexpected comments based on a customer's buying history.

- If you ask AI to evaluate teachers based on student grades, it could end up rewarding teachers who game the system and terminate honest ones unless you train it to value students' growth and improvement as much as the ultimate test scores.

It's become obvious that humans need to start teaching AI how to make good decisions aligned with a very clear set of values, or we will all have a lot of problems. The question is, whose values? Aligning AI's core values with those of humans will be an undertaking for policymakers, software developers, and society at large.

But when it comes to how you lead your new strategy, your first and most important responsibility is to understand your *own* personal values. Otherwise, you could end up taking shortcuts just as disastrous as a self-driving car running over pedestrians.

Your values guide how you evaluate options and make decisions every day. In fact, the root word of *evaluate* is the Latin word *valere*, which means "to be of value, to be worthy."

I regularly see boards and leadership teams assume that they have common values. Yet they don't take the time to clarify them or to seriously consider how they will apply them. Sure, they may brainstorm some nice words, put them on conference room walls, and splash them all over their website. Words like "honesty," "integrity," and "respect" may sound inspiring.

However, until you incorporate your values into the way you work, you are not aligned. This lack of alignment results in inconsistent decision making, confusion, skepticism, and frustration among the ranks. It also erodes credibility and trust.

Clear Values Make Decisions Easier

When you're in the leadership hot seat, making tough trade-offs every day, decision making can be arduous and stressful. Clear values help you prioritize and make decisions more easily and with integrity. Your "yes" can mean "*Yes!*" and your "no" can mean "*No!*" without the stress of second-guessing yourself.

Children who grow up in families with a clear set of values are able to navigate difficult decisions more confidently. In the same way, people facing difficult decisions on the front lines can make the right decisions more easily when your organization's core values are clearly defined. It requires open discussions about how your values should be applied in different real-world situations.

Clear Values Attract the Right People

Research shows that values (especially honesty, integrity, respect, and well-being) are more important to workers than most other considerations, including pay. More than half of US employees would be willing to take less pay in order to work at an organization whose values align with their own.[33]

Another study reported that over 70% of respondents, from nearly every age group, region, company size, and demographic group, say their employer has the obligation to be "a force for good."[34] Purpose-led organizations have to work especially hard at communicating their values and training people to live them out, encouraging values-based decision making that not only considers revenues and profit but the impact decisions have on people, the planet, and eternity.

Yet the motives of purpose-driven leaders are often questioned. Even well-intended efforts to drive impact can be met with skepticism and perceived as "virtue signaling" or "greenwashing." If you are going to step into the "doing good" game, you'd better be ready to be accountable.

Living Out Values Requires Being Intentional

Defining a clear purpose will attract people to join you. But don't expect people to stay engaged unless you are committed to living out that purpose. It starts with the leader.

The Nehemiah Entrepreneurship Community is a global non-profit that equips entrepreneurs to build businesses grounded in their values and faith. They guide every founder to invest the time up front to clarify their life purpose and values—even *before* drafting a business plan! The idea is that by knowing your personal values and making sure your business strategy is aligned with those values right from the start, you will make decisions more easily, lead others with integrity, enjoy your work more, and navigate the roller coaster of driving your strategy grounded in what matters most.

Getting clear on your values requires reflection. Here are two tools I've found to be helpful:

- A fun way to think through your values is by playing cards! Instead of starting with a blank piece of paper, the *Live Your Values Deck: Sort Out, Honor and Practice What Matters Most to You* is an actual deck of cards that helps consider which of seventy-three values resonates most with you and provides ideas of how each value applies in the real world. The deck can also be used as a group exercise to foster conversations about what your organization values most.

- Pam and Tom Wolf's book *Identity and Destiny: 7 Steps to a Purpose-Filled Life* is a thought-provoking workbook that systematically guides you through discovering your God-given purpose. You examine your unique gifts, personality, and resilience profiles as well as your passions, faith, and values. Group discussions using this workbook can be life-changing.

The time you invest in clarifying your own values and purpose is one of the best investments you can make to prepare you to lead others with integrity.

Put Your Values to Work

> *Just as your car runs more smoothly and requires less energy to go faster and farther when the wheels are in alignment, you perform better when your thoughts, feelings, emotions, goals, and values are in balance.*
> Brian Tracy, public speaker and self-development author

After you are clear on your values, both as an individual and as an organization, it's time to integrate them into how you work. Make them visible and frequently remind people of what your values are—*but don't stop there!*

Show specifically how to *use* your values in decision making. Incorporate them into your onboarding, role descriptions, sales process, vendor and partner agreements, performance reviews, and leadership development programs. Reference your values when you explain *how we do things here*.

Leaders can point out, "Because one of our values is (this), we do (that)." For example, "Because we value open communication, we hold quarterly town halls to talk about what is on people's minds as well as discuss the risks and opportunities we need to be ready for." Or "Because one of our core values is integrity, we went back and refunded all the customers that were impacted by our error."

Your values can serve as a north star everyone can find when they get stuck. When faced with a difficult decision, the alternative that best aligns with your organization's values will become the easiest choice.

Aligned to Make Progress Faster

When people are aligned to accomplish a big idea, they will make progress faster. Though some days you may feel that getting people aligned is like fighting an uphill battle, you can do this! By defining your strategic destination, seeking diverse perspectives, clarifying responsibilities and authority, and courageously stepping up when change is needed, you've created a solid game plan. When you and your team are grounded in common values, it works even better.

As you work your Game Plan for Alignment, you will reduce anxiety, speed decisions, and enable people to create results faster—especially when you communicate to inspire them to action.

Section 4 Key Takeaways
Overdrive: Aligning for Maximum Traction

To get traction quickly for your new strategy, people need to be on the same page. A lack of alignment results in friction, wasted energy, and disappointing results and can easily derail your strategy. You need a Game Plan for Alignment.

- Defining a *clear, measurable destination* is the first step. When you have limited capacity, choose an initial destination that could have maximum *impact* with minimal *effort*. This will accelerate enthusiasm and build momentum.

- Make time for diverse views and spirited debate. Instead of telling people to "get on board," invite them to get on the same page with you and *involve them in shaping* your new strategy. People will feel more ownership.

- When you clarify up front *who needs to take which action*, you save time, energy, and frustration.

- Alignment isn't forever. You'll need to *continuously recalibrate*. Create a cadence for sensing what is changing in your environment and within your organization.

- Be ready to have *difficult conversations*. When a person is no longer the right fit for their role, don't ignore it. Addressing the problem can actually reduce anxiety for the individual and the team as you take on the elephant in the room and enable everyone to get back on one page.

- Decision making will be easier when you *clearly articulate your values* and integrate them into how your organization works. This also helps attract the right people to join you on your journey.

Section 4 Notes and Action Steps
Overdrive: Aligning for Maximum Traction

(Jot down two to three things that jumped out that you can quickly apply.)

_____

_____

_____

_____

_____

_____

_____

_____

_____

_____

_____

_____

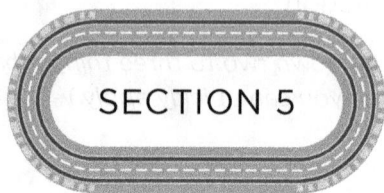

TURBOCHARGE: COMMUNICATING TO INSPIRE ACTION

If you can't communicate, it's like winking at a girl in the dark—nothing happens. You can have all the brainpower in the world, but you have to be able to transmit it. And the transmission is communication.

Warren Buffett, businessman, investor, and philanthropist

Even the hottest race car won't win if it never gets onto the track! In the same way, your new strategy will not succeed if people haven't heard about it or understood it.

In this section, we'll look at ways to share your carefully crafted strategy with a wider audience. In Chapter 15, we'll dig into the challenges of being heard in today's noisy environment and what you can do to overcome those challenges. In Chapters 16 and 17, we'll explore how to communicate your strategy so that people are ready to take action and examine the power of a consistent message.

In Chapters 18 and 19, we will explore how a Strategic Message Playbook can serve as your "single source of truth" to help you develop a powerful message and put it into action. By the end of this section, you'll have the tools you need to communicate so that people are prepared to take action with you. We'll start with understanding why people may not be listening.

CHAPTER 15

TODAY'S COMMUNICATION CONUNDRUM

When you're excited about your strategy, it can be frustrating if people don't immediately jump in and join you. I hear it all the time:

- The CEO called me, frustrated. He had been on the road, meeting with investors. "I carefully explain how what we offer will revolutionize the industry and how they can get in on the ground floor. But they just smile and say nothing. *Why don't they get it?*"

- The Executive Director called me, frustrated. She had been trying to get board approval to fund a new initiative. "This was the third time we reviewed this project, and they kept asking the same questions and putting off approving it. *Why don't they get it?*"

- The Program Manager called me, frustrated. He was following up with people who were overdue on deliverables. "We all agreed how critical this milestone was for our strategy. But they keep coming up with excuses for not taking action. *Why don't they get it?*"

When clients reach out to me for help, the problem they most often complain about is that people don't get their groundbreaking big idea. Getting the message right is crucial to create urgency and speed results. Why does it have to be so hard?

Can People Even Hear You?

In 1255 AD, the Dominican friar Vincent of Beauvais described the challenge of dealing with "the multitude of books, the shortness of time, and the slipperiness of memory . . ."[35]

More than 750 years later, Mike Allen and Jim VandeHei, the co-founders of media companies Axios and Politico, wrote in their book *Smart Brevity: The Power of Saying More with Less,* "Never in the history of humanity have we vomited more words in more places with more velocity . . . This new and exhausting phenomenon has jammed our inboxes, paralyzed our workplaces and clogged our minds."[36]

Information overload is not new. We just seem to be perfecting it! With our smartphones, online games, computers, TVs, smart kiosks, smart billboards, and e-books, in addition to reams of flashy print media, we are confronted today with a tsunami of words and visuals. It can be frustrating, and our brains don't like it.

Despite many of us bragging that we're great at it, research shows that humans don't actually multitask at all. Instead, we *switch* our attention between tasks, and in doing so, we make more mistakes.[37]

If our brains aren't shifting between the torrents of input, we're *shutting it out*. When we've had too much, our brains shut down and stop taking in information, a process scientists call "selective filtering."[38] Whether it's because of our slippery memories or clogged minds, we are filtering to survive in a tsunami of information. And there are consequences.

A Confused Mind Says No

Sometimes we filter out important information. We don't catch the correct time or gate number, and we miss a flight. We skip reading the financial gobbledygook in a contract, and we lose money. We don't hear the emotional nuance behind a comment, and a loved one's feelings are hurt. *As you try to share your big idea, people might filter you out too.*

When they don't hear or understand you, people get confused. And when people are confused, they don't take action. Decisions cause stress, and our brains are wired to protect us from stress. When we are confronted with confusing decision-making moments, our brains simplify our options to all-or-nothing extremes. The result is that we say no. When information overload and confusion meet, your strategy will stall.

When information overload and confusion meet, your strategy will stall.

People Only Focus When It Matters to Them

Have you ever clicked through hundreds of channels on the TV and complained, "There's nothing to watch!" Or stood in front of a refrigerator full of food and thought, "There's nothing to eat!" We may have multitudes of options, but unless a show or snack appeals to us right now, we dismiss it.

It's the same thing when it comes to the messages we hear. We get presented with loads of messages every day—just not ones we are interested in. We are filtering *out* more information every day than ever before.

But when we *do* see what we want, we focus on it and dig in! We can spend weekends binge-watching our favorite series or get so lost in a good book that we miss our stop on a train. Research shows that hard-core video gamers spend about eight-and-a-half hours playing each week.[39]

People can *hear you* when you provide information that *matters* to them *at that moment*!

Earlier, in Section 3, we discussed how each of us goes on a journey every time we make a decision. The Decision Makers' Journey starts with becoming aware we even have a problem, which requires that we consider all our options. Only then do we choose a solution and evaluate the benefits.

When you provide the right message to engage the right people at the right stage of their Decision Makers' Journey, they can actually *hear you*!

CHAPTER 16

COMMUNICATING TO MOVE PEOPLE TO ACTION

What exactly are you trying to communicate about your strategy? Leaders sometimes get confused about what they're trying to achieve. Do you just want to inform, or are you actually looking for people to *do* something?

An Invitation to Take Action

My friend Taly Walsh is masterful at inspiring people to accomplish a bigger purpose. Her ability to enlist people to do something new has always amazed me. Whether she's inviting people to get involved in a new industry collaboration or helping develop the workforce of the future, everyone always seems to say, "Yes."

Taly's office was down the hall from mine for a while, and I'd listen to her engage with people. She started by checking in about the other person's latest challenges or celebrating their victories. She would talk about the initiative she was working on, how excited she was about the impact it could have, and how the person on the other end of the phone would benefit too.

Then she invited the listener to take a specific next step: Attend! Bring someone! Join! Sponsor! Invest! Taly always ended with, "It'll be fun!" And people consistently said, "Yes!" and joined in enthusiastically.

I don't know if she did it consciously, but Taly consistently addressed four critical points when trying to motivate people to take action. These are exactly the four points Bert Decker realized he was missing when he completely bombed at pitching investors on his half-a-million-dollar idea for a new film. Bert turned his humbling experience into a quest to learn everything he could about communicating effectively. He discovered that our limbic brain (the nonreasoning, nonrational, subconscious, primitive part of our brain) acts as a filter for every single message we hear. It's trying to protect us, and to get past that filter, our communication needs to connect emotionally with the audience.

Bert realized that "self-centered" communication doesn't motivate people; only "audience-centered" content inspires people to take action. To achieve audience-centered communication, we need to always include these four points (that are part of the Decker Grid®):

1. Start with the *Listener's Perspective*. What do they know, understand, believe, and feel about the problem you are solving?

2. Have a clear *Point of View*. This is your own line in the sand about the problem. This doesn't waver, no matter who you are talking to. Your conviction and personal commitment to this point of view builds trust!

3. Establish a specific *Call to Action*. If you want people to act, you need to tell them what to do next! Not just big, lofty calls to "embrace a new direction," but specific next steps they can take easily.

4. Define the *Benefit of Taking Action*. As people are listening, WIIFM (what's in it for me?) is running through their heads. Provide the answer so they can focus on what you're saying.[40]

Realizing that audience-centered communication could change the game led Bert to start Decker Communications, a coaching and training firm that helps rising stars reach their full potential. The firm's next-generation leaders, co-CEOs Ben and Kelly Decker, have embraced the urgency of their mission. As they share in their book, *Communicate to Influence: How to Inspire Your Audience to Action*, people are begging to be inspired. It's never been more important to take a risk and change the way we communicate.

And it all starts with shifting our messages from "all about me" to audience-centered content that drives action.

Are You Slapping on a Coat of Paint?

At times, I've seen senior leaders get so excited about their new strategy and the potential impact they can make in the world that they suddenly proclaim, "We need to change our brand!"

They'll start noodling new names and logos and taglines. The excitement starts to build, and before you know it, they are changing their website and making a press release. "Hey! We're doing something new!"

Expecting a new name or logo alone to drive a new strategy just built in a boardroom is like slapping a coat of paint on an old station wagon and expecting people to think you have a high-powered race car! It's not authentic.

The day after your big, splashy announcement, a customer or funder is going to talk to someone in your organization or to one of your partners. When the person on the front line has no idea what this splashy new brand is about, or people's personal experience working with your organization is inconsistent with the new image you are trying to portray, you invite skepticism.

Before we go any further, let's get clear about the three building blocks of a new strategy that often get confused: *positioning, messaging,* and *branding.*

- **Positioning** is all about *you!* It clarifies your WHY and WHY YOU. It reflects who you are, your unique identity, what you stand for, who you serve, and the outcomes you deliver. Positioning is your foundation. It doesn't change, no matter who you talk to. When you start with strategic positioning, communication becomes much easier.

- **Messaging** is all about *them*! Messaging *connects* your positioning to those you serve with language that resonates. It starts with fully understanding the people you want to communicate with and how you can help them solve a problem or meet a need from *their* point of view. Your positioning may stay the same, but how you message can vary depending on the audience you are trying to reach, to ensure you are speaking in their language and terminology.

- **Branding** is about how your organization *looks* and *feels* when others interact with you. The term brand originally referred to an identifying mark to show ownership (like the brand ranchers put on their livestock). But in this age of social media and online connection, the concept of brands has evolved. Your brand is an opportunity to build relationships and grow loyalty. Through your logo, tagline, tone of voice, vocabulary, colors, fonts, and imagery, you can connect with your audience. But remember, branding has to be grounded in your strategic positioning, or it's not going to feel authentic.

> *Positioning is all about* you. *Messaging is all about* them. *Branding is how your organization* looks *and* feels *when others interact with* you.

By aligning these three building blocks—positioning, messaging, and branding—you will be able to communicate more effectively. When they are out of sync, your strategy will get stalled. When used in an intentional, coordinated way, they can help people hear you. Your strategy will come to life and more effectively move people to action.

Only when your organization starts to *live out your new strategy* is it time for a splashy brand change! By that point, your brand is more than a thin coat of paint. Your new brand is a public recognition of what you stand for and are already becoming. Your people can authentically talk about your direction, with proof points that you are on your way. The result? Your brand promise will be authentic and serve as the basis for genuine relationships built on trust.

One way you can maintain that trust is by making sure you communicate consistently.

CHAPTER 17

THE POWER OF CONSISTENCY

When you lead a team or an organization, it can be challenging to get everyone to deliver a consistent message. Consider these frustrated leaders:

> "When I meet personally with investors, they seem to understand our strategy. But when they talk to our team, they get totally confused about what we do!"
> —CEO of a startup

> "After all our work to get our message out through social media, mailings, and events, prospective donors still ask, 'What do you do?'"
> —Executive Director of a nonprofit

> "When we launched our latest offering, we provided a ton of information. But when I visit the regions, they seem to be selling products we don't even make!"
> —Product Manager of a tech company

Getting everyone on the same page at the outset of a new project is hard. But getting people to communicate the same message over time can be even more frustrating!

It's Worth Repeating

The public safety world has known this for years: Keep the message clear. Repeat it often. That way, in moments of stress, people will know what to do.

"Buckle Your Seat Belt!"
"Stop, Drop, and Roll!"
"See Something, Say Something!"

If you want everyone on the same page, employ this same public safety tactic. Though communicating the same message over and over again may *feel* boring, repetition helps people understand your message and prepares them to take action. After all, the more frequently you send the same message, the higher the odds people will *hear* you over the torrents of other noisy messages they are bombarded with every day.

Another advantage may be the "mere-exposure effect" framed by psychologist Robert Zajonc. His research indicates people tend to prefer a familiar idea over others. When they do, they are more likely to act.[41]

Repeatedly sending a consistent message can help move people to action, even if the people don't work for you! Research shows that managers who sent the same message repeatedly through many different media (email, text, conversations) got better and more timely responses from their teams. And even when leaders didn't have direct reporting authority (such as program or project managers), the most successful ones tended to be the most proactive and strategic about sending repeated messages to their cross-functional teams. Consistency works![42]

I've found that a regular communication drumbeat is especially critical during mergers and acquisitions. When people are uncertain about changes all around them, they often freeze. Leaders at every level need to be able to consistently communicate the Why and the desired outcome for the merger and connect the dots so people can understand how their own actions could help achieve the new strategy. Communicating frequently with a consistent message helps people get beyond their fear and starts to build trust. Only then will people be able to move forward and take action.

Former LinkedIn CEO Jeff Weiner is a big believer in the need for consistent communication when driving a new strategy. In an interview with *Business Insider*, Weiner explained,

You invest very heavily and thoughtfully in deciding what kind of company you want to be. And then you repeat it, over and over and over again. A friend of mine once paraphrased David Gergen, on the subject of repetition, "If you want to get your point across, especially to a broader audience, you need to repeat yourself so often, you get sick of hearing yourself say it. And only then will people begin to internalize what you're saying."[43]

To ensure a new strategy sticks, it's important people understand it. Don't miss these three steps:

1. Start with clear strategic positioning.
2. Define messages that are relevant to the audience.
3. Communicate consistently.

If you don't achieve all three, people won't get it. The results can be disastrous.

A Scrambled Message Spells Disaster

In 1999, NASA's Mars Climate Orbiter completed a ten-month journey into space with the mission of helping understand the history of water on Mars and the potential for life on the planet. On September 23, hundreds of scientists who had been consumed by this project for years were ready to celebrate the craft's entry into Mars's orbit.[44]

Instead, the spacecraft veered dangerously close to the planet's atmosphere where the $125M Orbiter burned up and broke into pieces. Why? An investigation found that it came down to communication.

One engineering team in Colorado used *metric* units (e.g., centimeters) while another team in California used *English* units (e.g., inches). Critical information for maneuvering the spacecraft into orbit got scrambled, killing the mission.

The consequences for scrambling messages in your organization may not be as severe or as costly as what happened to the Mars Orbiter. But when people are not able to communicate the right message at the right time, there's a risk your strategy might crash and burn too.

CHAPTER 18

YOUR ACCELERATION ADVANTAGE™: A STRATEGIC MESSAGE PLAYBOOK

What if everyone in your organization had the *right message* for the *right people* at the *right time* in one place? Your team could:

- Consistently explain what you offer and why your organization is different from others

- Be clear about who your target markets are (and aren't) and better prioritize their time

- Consistently use language that resonates with target audiences in writing or in conversations

- Communicate independently and be more productive, confident that they are on message without having to ask for approval.

> *When everyone has the* right *message at the* right *time for the* right *audience, your strategy will move faster.*

When everyone has the right message at the right time for the right audience, your strategy will move faster. Those you serve can understand your offering, whether they are talking to people on the front line or in the back office.

A Single Source of Truth: Your Strategic Message Playbook

One of the four success factors you need to create an ACCELERATION ADVANTAGE™ is consistent *communication* that moves people to action. A Strategic Message Playbook can help you communicate more powerfully. It synthesizes the key information about your strategic position and addresses the concerns of different audiences in one place so that you and your team can communicate consistently and confidently.

This "single source of truth" can help you create results faster. The key is to capture the right messages in one place so that everyone on your team can easily draw from them. They won't

The ACCELERATION ADVANTAGE™
Go to Market Impact LLC

have to scramble through old emails and PowerPoints or hesitate because they are unsure what to say.

An effective strategy cannot be developed in a vacuum. In the same way, the messages that reflect your strategic positioning cannot be built by one person or delegated to one department. To build your Strategic Message Playbook, you need to tap a team with diverse perspectives: different functions and roles, backgrounds, and geographies; front office and back office; bosses and frontline; newbies and seasoned pros. Ask each to come willing to share what they know as well as to listen and learn.

Planning for a diversity of thinking right from the start ensures that you'll examine the problem you solve from all angles and touchpoints and develop a message that will more likely resonate with your target decision makers.

Building your Strategic Message Playbook doesn't have to be complicated. I've provided a Strategic Message Playbook Template to help you start. It leverages the work you've already done in earlier sections of the book. Your task will be to synthesize these ideas into simple statements.

Focus first on defining your Positioning and your Value, which you'll want all of your audiences to know. Then capture unique messages that resonate with specific target segments or decision makers.

Don't worry about getting the message perfect. This is a work in process! Start with your best answers for now and try it on with real people to get feedback. Your Strategic Message Playbook is a living document that will continue to evolve based on the questions and feedback you get and what resonates most with different audiences.

THE STRATEGIC MESSAGE PLAYBOOK TEMPLATE

This template helps you synthesize key information about your strategy in one place so you and your team can communicate consistently and confidently. You can find a guide at bonus.fasttrackyourbigidea.com to help you build your own Strategic Message Playbook.

Our Positioning in the Marketplace

- The big problem we believe must be solved is *(your* WHY*)*.
- It is important to solve this problem now because *(your* WHY NOW*)*.
- Once this problem is solved, the result will be *(your vision)*.
- The top challenges to solving this problem are *(list all challenges)*.
- Our organization is focused on solving *(your specific niche)*.

Our Value

- We are on a mission to *(the high-level impact to be achieved)*.
- We are focused on serving *(specific target audiences/segments)*.
- What makes us unique is (WHY YOU/*list your differentiators)*.
- You can count on us to deliver *(measurable outcomes)*.

For Target Audiences

- We know you face unique challenges, such as *(pain points)*.
- We can address your unique needs by *(examples)*.
- You can have confidence choosing us because *(differentiators for this audience)*.

CHAPTER 19

PUTTING A STRATEGIC MESSAGE PLAYBOOK INTO ACTION

A Strategic Message Playbook can be a powerful tool. I've used this "single source of truth" with organizations large and small to accelerate results and move people forward. It works. Here are a few examples:

- Keeping People in the Know for a Complex Launch

  When I was part of a team launching a new product, new pricing structure, and new tools (all at the same time!), we knew it was going to be a challenge. We identified the myriad of audiences we needed to reach and what they each needed to know: sales, service, customer support, finance, manufacturing, partners, current customers and prospects, and press and industry analysts.

  The Strategic Message Playbook helped us equip our internal teams first so that everyone was on one page with a common understanding and message prior to the launch. Then, after we launched, the playbook served as a living document as we worked with external audiences, updating it as we got feedback. Despite the complexity, people across many different functions felt in the know and more confident.

- Equipping a Small Team to Move Faster

  An early-stage startup was on a mission to disrupt the market. But as the company quickly grew, the

CEO realized they needed to be more consistent about communicating their strategy. Their small team wasn't sending the same message when speaking to customers, prospects, investors, partners, and vendors, and they were confusing people.

When we worked to build their Strategic Message Playbook, we started with everyone sharing their different perspectives. Their insights were a treasure trove of differentiators, but they'd been using inconsistent language. We worked to clarify their strategic positioning and frame their unique value in a more cohesive way. They quickly created a shared language that everyone believed in and could use day-to-day.

- Accelerating Trust on Day One

  When an organization with a lot of product lines decided to spin out a division to be a standalone company, we knew there would be questions and confusion from employees and the marketplace: "Why are you doing this? What problem does this new company solve? Why now?"

  We developed a Strategic Message Playbook by systematically thinking through each audience's questions. We not only used these messages to prepare the press releases, website, and marketing materials, but we also used it to equip all the front-facing employees to talk about the company consistently on Day One. We even prepared the sales teams to explain our new strategy on a napkin!

Building Your Own Strategic Message Playbook

When you bring people together to build strategic messaging, it's going to take more than wordsmithing. You are going to be doing some heavy lifting: a combination of reflective thinking, honest dialogue, insights, negotiation, and a little fun thrown in.

Before you start, it's important to make sure everyone is at least familiar with the key concepts of your strategy and strategic messaging. (You could start by sharing this book as a pre-reading assignment for your team!)

Then ask each person to write down their own answers using the Strategic Message Playbook Template. (No PowerPoints, acronyms, or complicated diagrams are allowed!) Only after you consolidate the input and give everyone a chance to digest it will you bring everyone together to discuss it.

Most leaders are amazed we can actually get a group of diverse people with strong opinions to come together and agree in such a short period of time! But there are always a lot of "ah-ha" moments:

> "I was surprised by how many different perspectives our team had about our strategy. It was exciting to realize we can bring value in so many ways. I'm more comfortable talking about what we do."
>
> —Board Member

> "It was harder work than I thought it would be. Looking at things from our customers' point of view and trying to understand their problems, wants, and needs was a learning experience I will use as I develop new features or prioritize our development efforts."
>
> —Director of Research and Development

> "I appreciated that my input was considered in this process. I usually get talked over, so I was pleasantly surprised some of my ideas are part of the final message. And now I think I can finally explain to my family what this organization does!"
>
> —Finance Director

> "Now that we're clear on where we are going to focus and our niche, I'm much more confident explaining what we can actually deliver and why we're different. This is definitely going to be useful in customer conversations."
>
> —Head of Sales

Individuals I've worked with from organizations of all sizes and industries consistently report that defining their strategic messaging leads to new insights, clearer strategies, and better team alignment. Don't wait—start building your Strategic Message Playbook today and unlock these benefits for your team.

Building Trust, Inspiring Action

Communication is a powerful factor in creating an ACCELERATION ADVANTAGE™. Using the tools and concepts we've explored in this section, you are equipped to build a Strategic Message Playbook to communicate your strategy in a compelling way and inspire people to take action faster.

Communication will become even more important when you need to adapt to challenges down the road.

Section 5 Key Takeaways
Turbocharge: Communicating to
Inspire Action

To achieve your big idea, communicate so people understand and are prepared to take action.

- *A confused mind says no.* When information overload and confusion meet, your strategy will get stuck.

- Instead of *informing* people, you need to *inspire* them to take action. Audience-centered communication helps people understand your strategy and why they should join you.

- When you provide the *right information* at the *right time*, you can help people move forward faster and build trust.

- Your *strategic positioning* is the foundation of your strategy, your message, and your brand. It clarifies who you are, your unique identity, what you stand for, who you serve, and the outcomes you deliver. Your positioning doesn't change no matter who you talk to.

- *Audiences are different.* You may need to frame a message slightly differently to be relevant or appear sensitive to different audiences. Providing relevant examples and addressing common objections up front speeds their understanding.

- A simple message *repeated consistently* helps people understand faster and prepares them to take action.

- A Strategic Message Playbook can serve as your *"single source of truth."* It helps you and your team consistently and confidently communicate to accelerate results.

Section 5 Notes and Action Steps
Turbocharge: Communicating to Inspire Action

(Jot down two to three things that jumped out that you can quickly apply.)

_____

_____

_____

_____

_____

_____

_____

_____

_____

_____

_____

_____

_____

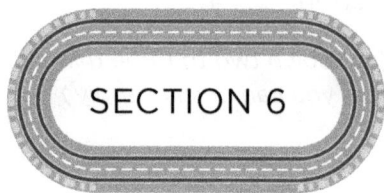

SHIFTING GEARS: ADAPTING TO PROPEL RESULTS

Adapt or perish, now as ever, is nature's inexorable imperative.
H.G. Wells, British novelist and short story writer

Once upon a time, Clark Griswold planned a trip to the Walley World amusement park, hoping it would be an opportunity to bond with his family. As they traveled across the country, though, they experienced mechanical problems, vandals, a car crash, and the deaths of their pet and their grandmother—only to find that Walley World was closed when they got there.

The plot of the movie *National Lampoon's Vacation* may sound farfetched, but if you are in the middle of implementing a new strategy, you may relate! Things rarely go as planned.

This section explores how you and your organization can adapt quickly to surprises. You'll learn to evaluate problems and create an Adaptive Roadmap to be ready for whatever is around the bend. Building on your de-risking work from Section 3, you'll be able to apply these principles to navigate and manage risks as they unfold. By the time you're finished, you'll be equipped to handle the bumpy roads ahead—and even look forward to them!

CHAPTER 20

An Uncertain Road Will Get Bumpy

Leading people in a new direction can be challenging. Every new strategy is full of uncertainty, and there will inevitably be surprises—for you as the leader and for the people who come with you on the journey. You and your organization must be ready to adapt.

In this chapter, you'll see why being able to quickly adapt as an organization is so crucial. You'll be introduced to specific tools you and your team can use to make adapting a regular part of how you work. And you'll learn how to create an Adaptive Advantage that will set you apart.

Surprises Are Inevitable—Some Are More Prepared Than Others

You may already know that the skin of a chameleon changes color to blend in as it moves from one environment to another. But did you know a chameleon can also rotate its eyes nearly 180 degrees, entirely independently from each other? Rotating eyes enable chameleons to focus on what they are doing at the moment while scanning for approaching predators.

Chameleons are also the only animals on Earth with completely horizontal feet. Their toes stick straight out on either side of their soles and wrap around branches. This enables chameleons to hold on tight when one slip off a branch could mean disaster!

In nature, many species, like the chameleon, are prepared to adapt to new situations so they can survive. But what about organizations? How well do they adapt to a changing environment? It turns out, not very well.

As Alan Iny and his team at the Boston Consulting Group observed, "Most companies haven't built the capabilities to manage, much less thrive, amidst uncertainty."[45]

Adapting isn't accomplished with one silver bullet. It requires that we continually modify our approach to fluctuating circumstances. It's not always straightforward or easy to adapt. That's because adaptive problems are different than most of the other problems you deal with on a daily basis.

Technical Problems vs. Adaptive Problems

To become good at adapting, you need to be ready for *adaptive problems*, not just technical ones. Technical problems are those that can be clearly defined and resolved, with solutions and skills that are available and proven. For instance, if your car isn't drivable because you have a flat tire, you've got a technical problem. Technical problems require pinpointing the issue (Which tire is flat?), matching existing solutions to the problem (Do you have a spare?), and getting the right resources to execute (Where can you get a new set of tires?).

But *adaptive* problems are still unfolding, so there's no quick fix. Say your family car is continually breaking down. If the problem is due to how your family uses your car, no number of trips to the mechanic will make things better. You and your spouse may be cautiously riding the brakes, overheating the brake pads as you do. Your aggressive teenager may accelerate and then hit the brakes hard, causing excessive wear. To solve this problem, all the drivers in the house are going to need to adapt how they drive.

The root cause of an adaptive problem is unclear, and the solution is hard to pin down. Multiple stakeholders own the responsibility for an adaptive problem, and solving it requires everyone to change both their mindsets and behaviors. You will recognize you have an adaptive problem when you start to see recurring crises and persistent conflicts.

Adaptive problems for an organization could show up as:

- An increase in employee resignations
- Increased return rates due to customer complaints about quality
- Disappointing sales of a new offering
- Difficulties meeting a sudden increase in demand.

Many leaders try to take charge by quickly throwing technical solutions at an adaptive problem. This is an understandable instinct, but it can actually make things worse. Even your biggest supporters can become disillusioned when they see you throwing time and money at a problem without fixing it.

Getting really good at solving adaptive problems requires stepping back, thinking more broadly, asking more questions, and changing your mindset about how to approach the problem. It also requires involving people to adapt to a new way of working and moving forward together.

Adapting Quickly Creates a Competitive Advantage

In stable times, organizations can grow by getting more efficient at what they are already doing. But in an unpredictable environment, organizations that do what they've always done can become irrelevant. New priorities and competitors emerge. Customers, employees, volunteers, and funders want to solve problems in new ways—and can move on without you if you're not willing to adapt. It comes down to developing a system to adapt.

Scientist and strategist Joerg Esser suggests:

> The real issue is not successfully transforming your organization on a one-time basis—it's writing the ability to adapt and transform into the company's

DNA. It's developing a mechanism or reflex for dealing with whatever crisis comes along, be it financial, technological, environmental, or health-related.[46]

How can you make sure that the ability to adapt is part of your own organization's DNA? Let's explore ways you can build a system to create a more adaptive organization.

CHAPTER 21

Your
Acceleration Advantage™:
An Adaptive Roadmap

Imagine you are driving a car late at night down a two-lane road. Traffic is light. The moon is full and shining brightly. You turn on some music and enjoy the scenery.

A deer suddenly darts out on the road as you come around a bend. At the same moment, another car comes toward you! In a split second, you become focused, evaluate the situation, and adapt your course to avoid a collision with either the deer or the other car.

In that crucial moment, you quickly apply a variety of skills you first learned as a new driver: you brake, swerve, and lay on the horn to alert the other driver. Because you have years of experience driving, you're able to seamlessly put it all to work in an emergency situation.

If you're responsible for leading a new strategy, you need to be able to adapt quickly too. You must recognize what has changed, use your capabilities and strengths in new ways, and shift your course to address difficult challenges. The trick is to develop these abilities before crises hit, providing the leader an inner roadmap that becomes instinctive.

But it is one thing to be able to adapt as an *individual*; it's a much bigger challenge for an organization or an entire *ecosystem* to be able to steer quickly around disruption. How can you avoid the confusion, finger-pointing, and fear that destabilizes so many teams and partnerships when confronted with surprises?

I've found that leaders and organizations who adapt quickly seem to have developed an inner "roadmap" to navigate disruption and *instinctively adapt together*.

To maintain momentum you will need to continually adapt. *Adapting* is one of the critical factors you need to create your ACCELERATION ADVANTAGE™. By consistently applying three principles, you and your team can create an "Adaptive Roadmap" for your organization. This roadmap will help you and others more objectively evaluate the situation, remain calm, see options amidst the disruption, and stay on course to continue executing your strategy together.

The three principles of your Adaptive Roadmap are:

- Principle #1: Build an adaptive mindset.

- Principle #2: Take imperfect action.

- Principle #3: Lead with your strengths.

Let's dive into how to leverage these principles as an individual and as an organization. Building an Adaptive Roadmap right from the start will help you and your team more confidently deal with the bumpy roads ahead.

The ACCELERATION ADVANTAGE™
Go to Market Impact LLC

ADAPTIVE PRINCIPLE #1

BUILD AN ADAPTIVE MINDSET

*Those who cannot change their minds
cannot change anything.*
George Bernard Shaw, Irish playwright,
critic, and political activist

*Do not conform to the pattern of this world
but be transformed by the renewing of your mind.*
Romans 12:2 (NIV)

Your mindset is the set of beliefs that shapes how you make sense of the world. It influences how you think, feel, and behave in any given situation—which, in turn, determines how you behave when confronted with change. An organization's mindset is the sum of all its members' beliefs and thoughts, which shapes the organization's culture.

An *adaptive mindset* is able to evaluate change with less fear and move toward seeing solutions. An adaptive mindset helps you avoid the fight-or-flight reaction of the "old brain" and be open to new opportunities. An organization with an adaptive mindset can align quickly, adapt to disruptive situations, and move forward together. It creates *resilience*.

One way to help your organization embrace an adaptive mindset is to ensure your WHY can endure over time.

Reconfirm an Enduring WHY

The foundation of your strategy begins with your WHY, the problem you solve. A key principle in the DE-RISK SYSTEM FOR IMPACT® (Section 3) is to not just be clear on your WHY but understand WHY NOW. This reduces risk by ensuring the problem you aim to solve is relevant and urgent.

However, after you've set your course and launched your big idea, the world doesn't stop! Technology, regulation, competition, and social issues constantly change. Your

WHY can inspire you and others to see roadblocks as inconveniences instead of insurmountable obstacles. It can also motivate you to devise entirely new ways to accomplish your mission.

Given the effects of COVID-19, the entire business world is now familiar with "pivoting" or steering an organization through a profound shift in strategy. While many startups recognize the need to pivot, this concept is now seen as a core skill for established businesses as well. When you and your team are clear on your WHY and solving an enduring problem, you are able to stay less attached to one specific tactic. You can more easily see options and change the approach you use to achieve your goal.

Netflix is an excellent example of a company that defined a big WHY. They revolutionized the business of film and television—completely. In the late 1990s, founders Reed Hastings and Marc Randolph had a big idea: to become the best entertainment distribution service in the world. They started Netflix by mailing DVDs to homes. When Internet technology was more mature, they pivoted to delivering movies with a streaming service. To attract a bigger audience, they pivoted again to start producing their own original entertainment content. Despite the market changing around them, their WHY was enduring enough to help Netflix leaders continually see opportunities and seize them. While the company has recently struggled to retain its massive subscriber base, I wouldn't count them out based on their innovative track record and enduring WHY.

Your WHY needs to be specific enough to inspire people to take action and big enough to endure over time.

When launching a new strategy, it's important to strike a balance. Your WHY needs to be *specific* enough to inspire people to take action and *big* enough to endure over time. If the problem you are focused on can easily be solved by a new technology or process, you may be confusing your WHY with "how."

Is Your WHY Big Enough?

Sometimes staying relevant requires expanding your WHY as you learn more about the problem you are working to solve. Goodwill Industries recognized this as they grew. In 1902, Reverend Edgar Helm, from the Morgan Methodist Church Chapel in Boston, started a nonprofit based on his belief in the power of work to improve lives. Goodwill's initial focus was to train people with disabilities to build skills and become more employable. Their mission was to help people secure jobs.

Over the years, however, Goodwill's leaders realized that helping people secure jobs was only one part of their much larger purpose: helping *communities* prosper. They saw a bigger vision for "a community where equitable access to career opportunities is available for all." The result was that Goodwill expanded its mission "to enhance the dignity and quality of life of individuals and families by strengthening communities, eliminating barriers to opportunity, and helping people in need reach their full potential through learning and the power of work."[47]

Goodwill Industries is now an independent network of over 150 community-based organizations around the world. Each local Goodwill chapter pursues the organization's WHY in different ways to ensure it addresses the priorities of its local community and remains relevant. In addition to offering job training for the disabled, local chapters may provide recruiting, staffing services, or daycare for disabled adults, offer job training for veterans, or even establish local manufacturing facilities to create local jobs. The organization is structured to flexibly innovate and adapt to the local community's needs, as each local chapter of Goodwill customizes "how" to pursue the bigger WHY.

Future-Proof Your WHY

Even as a startup, Netflix's WHY was big enough to stay relevant as market forces changed around them. Goodwill's WHY needed to expand as they learned more about the problem they solved. Both are examples of organizations that leveraged an adaptive mindset to accelerate results.

As you put your strategy into action, you will gain a deeper understanding of how it plays out in real-world scenarios. These insights provide glimpses into ways your own WHY might need to evolve and expand. To stretch your adaptive mindset, why not stress-test your WHY *today* to see how well it might endure into the future?

One way to do this is with the "WHY Later" Exercise. This exercise prepares you and your team for change and helps you examine the problem you solve in a new context.

You may be thinking, "Didn't we do a WHY exercise earlier?" Yes, in Section 3, you defined your "WHY/WHY NOW" Formula, a snapshot of the problem you solve today. But the "WHY Later" Exercise is a way to future-proof your strategy so that it remains *relevant over time*. It can help you and your team develop a more adaptive mindset—and have some fun!

By building an adaptive mindset, you and your team are equipped to move forward despite the inevitable disruption ahead, especially if you are willing to take imperfect action.

THE "WHY LATER" EXERCISE

The purpose of this exercise is to consider how well your current WHY will endure over time. It can also help you build a more adaptive mindset. Download the "WHY Later" Exercise at bonus.fasttrackyourbigidea.com.

1. Confirm Your Current WHY/WHY NOW Statement

- The problem we solve is *(pain point)* for *(our target audience)* to achieve *(desired outcomes)*.

- This problem is important to solve NOW because *(list of reasons)*.

- If this problem is *not* solved, *(list of consequences)*.

2. Time Travel: What Will Your WHY Look Like Later?

- *Imagine it's one hundred years from now.* Technology, competitors, and social issues have evolved. Will your target audience still have this same pain point? Is there anything about your current WHY NOW that will sound a little dated or even irrelevant?

- *If you expanded your geography or target market* tomorrow, how would your WHY statement need to change?

- *Imagine you have completely solved the pain point* you've been working on. What remaining issues might your target audience still be dealing with? Is there anything about your WHY that needs to evolve to address those issues?

3. What Can We Apply Today?

- List two to three areas where your WHY might need to adapt over time.

- What do you need to learn more about, and who can you ask?

- Put a plan in place to explore and a time to revisit this topic.

ADAPTIVE PRINCIPLE #2
Take Imperfect Action

Henry Ford had a big idea. He believed the average person should be able to experience the freedom and mobility of owning an automobile. In 1908, Ford Motor Company revolutionized the automobile industry with the Model T, which cost less than a third of the competition.

But did you know that Henry Ford's obsession with creating the perfect car almost *ruined* the company?

Ford spent years tweaking and perfecting the Model T. He wouldn't hear about creating another model until his Model T was perfected. He was resistant to feedback from his own employees and customers. His engineers threatened to quit. His obsession put strains on his family life. Competitors were introducing new alternatives to the Model T, and Ford's market share started to decline significantly. Even the world's greatest innovators can get stuck!

A changing environment means getting comfortable taking *imperfect action*. Imperfect action means making progress toward a goal with a small step. The step may not achieve your vision, but taking a few steps imperfectly is better than taking no action at all.

Think back to when you first learned to ride a bicycle. You weren't ready to enter the Tour de France yet. But you were ready to take imperfect action! Your first goal was to be able to sit on the bike without falling over. Though you may have been a little wobbly at first, you then took small actions to move the pedals forward and keep your balance, probably with some help. Then, despite a few spills, you proudly claimed victory and were ready to ride by yourself!

An organization that embraces imperfect action can also make progress in small steps. It can develop products faster, respond to market changes more quickly, and gain a competitive edge.

So how do you become more comfortable taking imperfect action? By getting on a bicycle! Here are three tips to help you and your team take imperfect action and get things done.

Establish Minimum Viable Objectives

Greatness from small beginnings (Sic Parvis Magna)
Favorite Latin motto of Sir Francis Drake, explorer and buccaneer

Most leaders want to launch their big new idea with a lot of fanfare and excitement. But when progress isn't going fast enough, the wind can quickly go out of everyone's sails—including the leaders'. People get frustrated. Morale tumbles. Momentum is lost.

Defining and implementing a strategy based on "minimum viable objectives" can help you learn faster what works and what doesn't!

The concept of the "Minimum Viable Project" (MVP) originated from the Lean Startup methodology developed by entrepreneur Eric Ries. The idea is to create a product or service with just enough features to test assumptions, gather customer feedback, and use that feedback to improve your offering.

This same approach applies equally well to your organization's goals, including those that don't directly relate to a product or service. For each of your strategic objectives, ask, "What is the minimum scope we can deliver that would have value? What can we learn if we achieve at least this minimum?" By achieving these minimum viable objectives, people will move forward faster, gaining confidence that you are taking the right direction.

Reward Taking Small Steps

The secret of getting ahead is getting started.
Mark Twain, author and humorist

A high-stakes strategy is complex. The consequences are significant, there usually aren't enough resources, and it always requires people do something new. It's common for individuals to get overwhelmed and freeze, fearful of taking any action at all.

People often overcome their fears by breaking a complex task down into smaller steps. But did you know you can actually "trick" your brain into taking small steps to make progress? In his book *Atomic Habits*, author James Clear shares four laws that help people change behavior. The first three laws increase the odds a person will perform the behavior: first, make it obvious; second, make it attractive; and third, make it easy. If all three of these conditions are met, you'll likely complete a task faster without having to think about it too much or coax yourself into it. But it's the fourth law that increases the odds that your brain will actually repeat the behavior next time: to make it satisfying![48]

Establishing a reward system, even for small steps, can help people move forward and develop a more adaptive mindset. The reward could be as simple as a quick walk or ringing a bell, or it could be a dinner out or plaque to recognize an important milestone. Reward getting started and make each step of progress more satisfying, then let your brain do the rest!

Establish a Return on Investment for Mistakes

Failure is only failure if it happens in the last chapter. Otherwise, it's a plot twist.

Danny Iny, educator, entrepreneur, and author

Have you ever heard that it's good to "fail fast"?

The "fail fast" concept is used in business, technology, and innovation circles to encourage rapid experimentation. Instead of avoiding failure at all costs, failing fast encourages people to take calculated risks, test hypotheses, and learn from the outcomes, whether they are successful or not.

But there's one problem. *Failing feels really bad!* When we make mistakes, our brains release stress hormones. We feel disappointment, embarrassment, even shame. Our fight-or-flight reflex makes us want to run and hide.

I remember sitting in a room full of executives from around the world, reviewing our year-end results. Many of us had performed below target.

Suddenly our leader stopped and said, "We're going to change things up today and talk about mistakes." The room got quiet. People looked at the floor. You could almost hear our fight-or-flight reflexes kicking in.

He continued, "Our new strategy requires we do things we've never tried before. Inevitably, we're all going to make mistakes. If we don't learn from our mistakes, all we do is incur the costs. So today, each of us is going to share one mistake we made this past year and what we are learning from it. I'll start."

And so began one of the best leadership development sessions I've ever been a part of. Each leader went through one mistake and the decisions that led to it. We shared the pain, the scars, and the learnings. We talked about how those learnings could apply to our own areas of responsibility. Suddenly, we weren't competing about whose numbers looked better. We morphed into a bunch of curious scientists and eager investors, learning together how to get the best return on our mistakes.

The return on investment for our mistakes is our learning. We've been taught since childhood that mistakes are bad. Flipping that idea on its head and seeing them as investments (even celebrating them as imperfect actions!) can help you get less attached to perfect outcomes.

> *The return on investment for our mistakes is our learning.*

Why not try holding an "ROI on Mistakes" conversation with your own team? Celebrate what you've learned. You will be surprised how this open communication can build trust and prepare your team to bounce back from mistakes so they can move on.

When you implement your strategy with an adaptive mind-set, you evaluate disruption with less fear. If you've done the work to ensure your mission is relevant over time and are comfortable taking imperfect action, you will be more prepared to lead, no matter what you encounter on the bumpy road ahead.

And if everyone on your team and all of your partners are actively working with you to develop adaptive mindsets, driving your strategy will be even easier.

But an adaptive mindset is just the start. You'll still need specific skills, experience, and expertise to maneuver the bumps. Let's consider how you can leverage them to fast track your strategy.

ADAPTIVE PRINCIPLE #3

LEAD WITH YOUR STRENGTHS

One morning, our kids hurried downstairs to make their lunches before school. They were met by their dad, who was not smiling. "Unfortunately, we're completely out of bread. No sandwiches today. What else can you take for lunch?" Confused, the kids waited for Dad to provide the answer. But he just looked back at them. "No, really!" he said. "Help me figure this out. The school bus is almost here. All hands on deck!"

Both children scoured the refrigerator and all the cabinets, searching for a solution. But no luck. "Just peanut butter isn't a lunch," grumbled my son. "Soup? I don't even know how to open a can!" worried his younger sister.

Suddenly, my husband declared, "I have an idea!" He placed two six-packs of soda on the counter, handed one to each kid, and said, *"Trade!"*

When they got home from school, both children were bubbling with excitement. "Best lunch ever!" "Let's do it again tomorrow!" "What else do we have that we can trade?"

My husband's approach (though admittedly unconventional parenting) focused our kids on what they *did* have instead of what they didn't. He changed the mindset of their small but mighty team to overcome the challenges of the day and move forward with confidence.

When a leadership team is under pressure to drive a new strategy, it's easy for them to fall into a scarcity trap. They worry, "We don't have enough time!" "We need more funding!" "There's no way we can do this without hiring more people!" Or worse, teams start to believe they don't have enough good ideas.

LEGO learned this the hard way. In the early 2000s, LEGO was almost bankrupt. Although its colorful bricks had been around since the 1950s, exciting new video games were winning kids' hearts and parents' wallets. The company's initial reaction was to innovate by imitating its competitors. It opened LEGO theme parks, LEGO jewelry, and LEGO clothing—but it lost even more money!

Enter a new leader, CEO Jørgen Vig Knudstorp. He challenged the LEGO team to refocus on their core strengths: "creative play" and "building experiences." They innovated with what they knew best and created a wider variety of ways to play with well-loved bricks. They invited their customers to innovate with them. And instead of trying to do everything themselves, LEGO partnered with experts in entertainment. They created exciting new building experiences with themes from TV shows like *The Simpsons* and movies like *Star Wars* and *Harry Potter*. The result? Within eleven years, LEGO had quadrupled its profits. Today, the LEGO brand ranks as one of the most highly regarded companies in the world as it continues to innovate, adapt, and evolve.

Focus on What You *Do* Have

This "strength-based approach" is based on a psychological therapy technique initially developed to help trauma victims. The approach is now applied in fields far beyond healthcare—education, employee development, parenting, sports coaching, and more.

The concept is simple: instead of focusing on how to fix all your weaknesses, start by focusing on what you do have: your strengths. This isn't just rah-rah. This is your brain at work. Consider the following:

- A McCraty study reported that participants who said they felt grateful for what they had showed a marked reduction in their level of a stress hormone called cortisol. Their hearts functioned better, and they were measurably more resilient to setbacks.[49]

- A National Institute of Health study using MRI scans of the brain discovered that feelings of genuine gratitude cause the brain to release a surge of dopamine. This chemical messenger helps regulate motivation, motor learning, and feelings of pleasure.[50]

- A study reported in the *Journal of Aging Research* found that having a sustained positive mental attitude was linked to decreased mortality.[51]

In my journey as an entrepreneur, my gratitude journal frequently helps me get unstuck and face the day with more confidence. This approach can equip entire organizations to take on new challenges more confidently.

Start your journey by focusing on what you do have.

Identify Your Strengths as Individuals

Strengths-based teamwork starts with understanding what everyone brings to the table. People are often unaware of their own strengths, much less the strengths and experiences of the people they work with every day.

There are many free and low-cost tools on the market to help you, your team, and your partners assess and understand your unique strengths and styles. (For a list of resources go to bonus.fasttrackyour bigidea.com.)

Understanding each team member's strengths can help you work together more effectively to resolve problems and adapt to change. These insights can also help ensure that people are in the right roles.

No One Is Perfect (But the Right Team Can Get Pretty Darn Close!)

When building a strategy for a high-stakes initiative, it is helpful to step back and evaluate the current situation. For decades, people have used a "SWOT" analysis, a strategic planning framework that helps visualize a project or an organization's Strengths, Weaknesses, Opportunities, and Threats (SWOT). Strengths and Weaknesses are internal factors, while Opportunities and Threats are *external* factors.

But I find a SWOT analysis can sometimes be a trap! Many teams can get lost in the analysis, frozen by all the threats and weaknesses and skeptical they can seize the opportunities. Sometimes, people finish the SWOT analysis more over-whelmed than motivated!

A SWOT Strategic Planning Framework

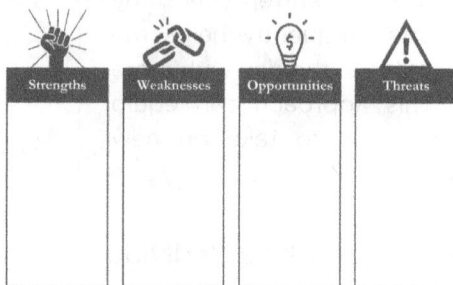

Strengths	Weaknesses	Opportunities	Threats

Here's a better way: *Before* you start a SWOT analysis, thoroughly brainstorm *every strength you have* as an organization that can equip you for your strategy journey. Individuals who are aware of all their strengths as a team will have a much easier time seeing opportunities. To ensure you are leading with all your strengths, go through the "Our Strengths Checklist" and add more of your own. Make a game of it. Bask in these strengths for a while, and *then* do the SWOT analysis. You'll find that when your team is grounded in their strengths, they can jump into the exercise with gusto. They will not only see more opportunities but will also be ready to conquer those scary threats and weaknesses like superheroes!

The Strengths of an Adaptive Ecosystem

An ecosystem is an interconnected community where members rely on others to create outcomes. Whether in nature or industry, ecosystems can be powerful yet complex. Industry ecosystems comprise a myriad of organizations—large and small, startups and established firms, buyers and suppliers, businesses and governments, nonprofits and communities. Leveraging the strengths of these diverse organizations can solve some of the world's biggest problems.

For these organizations to succeed over time, they must

work together comfortably and efficiently despite their differences. In our book, *The Maturity Stages of a Trusted Diverse Ecosystem*, diverse supply chain expert Ana Maria Lowry and I explore what it takes for adaptive ecosystems to thrive.

Our research found that industry and supplier ecosystems adapt together more quickly when they establish the building blocks of a robust strategy: framing a common purpose (WHY), clarifying a joint value proposition (WHY YOU), and defining standard operating models when they work together (RE-THINK HOW).

Most importantly, thriving adaptive ecosystems are built upon a critical shared strength: *common values* that inform how they work together and manage risk. Without shared values, trust breaks down and decisions get stuck.

For more information about building a diverse, trusted ecosystem, visit bonus.fasttrackyourbigidea.com.

OUR STRENGTHS CHECKLIST

Before doing a SWOT analysis, use this list as a guide to thoroughly brainstorm every strength you have as an organization. Visit bonus.fasttrackyourbigidea.com to download a copy of this checklist.

- Our employees' unique talents and strengths
- Our products and services, especially ones that have a loyal following
- Our systems and tools
- Our processes that we have refined to work well, especially those our competition may struggle with
- Our physical assets and inventories
- Our financial assets
- Our patents and other intellectual property
- Our research and unique market insights we've gathered over the years
- Our trusted customer relationships and interdependencies
- Our trusted partners
- Our trusted suppliers and contractors
- Our trusted funders
- Our community relationships
- Our government relationships
- Our relationships with others in the industry and across our ecosystem
- Our collective experiences and learnings (including our hard-won knowledge of what *doesn't* work!)
- Our reputation
- Other strengths *(challenge each other to come up with more!)*

Take One Day to Focus on What You *Do* Have

By focusing on the strengths and resources you do have, as well as the progress you are making, you can build positive momentum. It's not that the risks of your strategy suddenly disappear. But focusing on your strengths reveals new ways to see and redirect capacity so that you're working as smart as possible.

Every year, Americans and Canadians stop everything for one day to apply a strength-based approach. We call it "Thanksgiving." On that holiday, we intentionally and proudly prioritize being grateful for what we have.

Why not do the same for your team? Invest one day focusing on your strengths and creating a more confident organization ready to adapt to the challenges ahead. The results can be powerful.

When you lead with your strengths, embrace an adaptive mindset, and are ready to take imperfect action, you and your team will have created an Adaptive Roadmap. You will be able to navigate the risks and disruptions ahead more confidently.

The next question is this: Are you the right kind of leader?

CHAPTER 22
BECOMING AN ADAPTIVE LEADER

Frank Williams was the scrappy founder of a Formula 1 racing team struggling to make their way back to the top. One night, as Frank was driving to the airport, he came across a sharp turn in the road, hit a low stone wall, and dropped eight feet into the field below. Crushed under the roof, Frank's spine was fractured in two places. He would end up being paraplegic for the rest of his life.

But that did not stop Frank. Nor did it stop his team. According to a story by Damien Smith in *Motorsport* magazine, "To the rest of us, [Frank's] resilience in the face of such severe physical disability made him a figure of dumbfounding awe. To the man himself, it was just the reality he found himself living. Self-indulgence, self-pity? Not likely. After the accident, the only option was to press on regardless. That was the Williams way."[52]

Despite the many unknowns, Frank Williams inspired and challenged his team to become one of history's most-winning Formula 1 racing teams. His ability to adapt to adversity and invite his team to help shape a new chapter is a tribute to Williams' adaptive leadership.

Adaptive leadership is *not* about using authority or influence to *tell* people how to adapt. Adaptive leadership is about equipping and challenging people to courageously face a new problem so that they quickly understand it and can move forward to be part of solving it.

I like how authors Ronald Heifetz, Marty Linsky, and Alexander Grashow frame adaptive leadership in their book, *The Practice of Adaptive Leadership: Tools and Tactics for Changing Your Organization and the World*. Their definition of adaptive leadership is "marshaling people to tackle unknowns and thrive while you are doing it."[53] Are you challenging yourself to become a *thriving* adaptive leader?

I've listed ten questions to prompt your thinking about where you need to grow and adapt personally as a leader. The next step is action. Why not identify at least ONE area where you want to stretch as a more adaptive leader? As you develop the qualities of an adaptive leader, you are also making it easier for others to join and support you.

When Adapting Becomes Second Nature

Adapting is a survival skill for individuals and organizations. By putting an Adaptive Roadmap in place, you and your team can see options and move forward faster when you run into roadblocks.

We've explored tools and concepts to help you build an adaptive mindset, get comfortable taking imperfect action, and more consistently lead with your strengths. You are equipped to make adapting second nature so that it simply becomes *how we do things here.* As an adaptive leader, you are more prepared to take on the unknown. But you are also developing a courageous and inspired team to join you at every step.

ARE YOU AN ADAPTIVE LEADER?

Use these ten questions to prompt your thinking about where to grow personally as an adaptive leader. Why not identify one area in which you want to stretch your adaptive leadership muscles? Download a copy of these questions at bonus.fasttrackyourbigidea.com.

1. Do you invite others to shape the vision with you?

2. Are you comfortable admitting that you don't have all the answers?

3. Do you engage people to solve problems and lead the effort with you?

4. Do you listen with humility, acknowledging other perspectives have merit?

5. Are you willing to confront reality and listen to answers you don't want to hear?

6. Are you genuinely curious and open to learning as well as unlearning?

7. Are you comfortable stepping up to courageous conversations and openly discussing risks and mistakes—even your own?

8. Do you invite people to experiment and look for lessons in setbacks?

9. Do you consider plans from different points of view, with compassion for the people you are asking to make changes?

10. Do your actions support your values?

Section 6 Key Takeaways
Shifting Gears: Adapting to Propel
Results

To prepare for the bumpy road ahead, sustaining a new strategy demands you build an adaptive organization—starting with adaptive leaders.

- Organizations require an *Adaptive Roadmap* to quickly adapt to a changing environment and establish a competitive advantage. *Adaptive problems* are different from technical problems. Adaptive problems are still unfolding, and decisions must be made despite many unknowns.

- A person, team, or ecosystem that develops an *adaptive mindset* evaluates change with less fear and can quickly adapt together.

- Focusing on your organization's *strengths first,* rather than its gaps, will reveal possibilities you had never imagined. It will also build a more adaptive team.

- *Adaptive leadership* is not about telling people *how* to adapt. It is about equipping and challenging people to face a new problem courageously despite the unknowns so that they understand it and can move forward to be part of solving it.

Section 6 Notes and Action Steps
Shifting Gears: Adapting to Propel
Results

*(Jot down two to three things that jumped out
that you can quickly apply.)*

_____

_____

_____

_____

_____

_____

_____

_____

_____

_____

_____

_____

CONCLUSION

FAST TRACK YOUR STRATEGY TODAY

You're at the starting line, your heart pounding. Months of preparation have led to this moment. The flag drops and you accelerate, fueled by the possibilities. As you and your team celebrate at the finish line, you feel a rush of adrenaline and pride, having successfully executed your vision.

Ready for the Race

Steering your strategy to the finish line is a thrilling opportunity. You now have everything you need to create your own ACCELERATION ADVANTAGE™. You are equipped to:

- *De-risk* your strategy systematically.

- *Align* people to move forward together.

- *Communicate* your big idea so people are inspired to take action.

- *Adapt* quickly as a leader and as a team.

Yes, leading people in a new direction is challenging. You may not always be going as fast as you'd like. You may have even gotten off course at some point. But you no longer have to remain stuck on the sidelines.

What's Next?

The question for you now is this: What will you do next? Will you put this book down and think, "That was interesting. Somebody (*else*) should do that"?

You have the opportunity to step up and lead your strategy with more confidence than ever before and to bring others along with you.

Strategy Is a Team Sport

Use this book to invite people to think *with* you about navigating the risks to achieve your big idea. Whether you share it with your team, your board, your boss, a friend, or a coach, you can begin a dialogue that will spark momentum.

Set aside time to discuss and challenge each other. Try some of the exercises to get people thinking together. Tackle some of those difficult conversations you have been avoiding.

As you apply the principles in this book, you and your team will continue to gain more clarity. You have what you need to boldly consider the risks of your strategy, seize opportunities, and quickly address setbacks. As you put your strategic roadmap into action, you can more confidently lead others to shape the future.

Start Your Engines!

The world needs your big idea. Now it's time to make it a reality. Godspeed on your journey.

I look forward to celebrating with you at the finish line!

RESOURCES TO SUPPORT YOU ON YOUR JOURNEY

You may be framing a new strategy or getting one back on track. Your team may need a jump start or simply welcome a fresh perspective. Wherever you are along the way, I would be honored to support you to:

Take Your Best Next Step

Start by taking imperfect action. Go back and review the Action Steps you identified in each section and start putting your strategic roadmap into action. As you do, I'd love to come with you.

Dive into resources at bonus.fasttrackyourbigidea.com. There are exercises, templates, checklists, a glossary, and recommended reading if you want to dive deeper. Let me know what parts of this book resonated most, how you are using the book and resources, and which new topics you'd like to see addressed.

Support Your Team

If the concepts in this book resonate and you'd like me to support you, why not leverage my programs or 1:1 consulting? I am also available to speak and facilitate workshops at events and retreats. To learn more about my latest offerings, visit gotomarketimpact.com/offerings.

Share This Book

Start a dialogue by sharing this book with others. There are bulk discounts and special promotions when you order in volume directly at fasttrackyourbigidea.com.

Let's Connect!

I would love to hear about *your* big idea and the lessons you are learning!

Connect with me at:

- hello.susanschramm.com
- LinkedIn: www.linkedin.com/in/susanbaileyschramm

Download the
Fast Track Your Big Idea!
Bonus Resources
for FREE

BUILD A FLYWHEEL TO
MOVE YOUR STRATEGY FORWARD

You can create an ACCELERATION ADVANTAGE™ for your strategy. Download these free Fast Track bonus resources today.

You'll find exercises, templates, checklists, a glossary, and recommended readings, all designed to help you:
- **De-risk your strategy to avoid common mistakes**
- **Align people to reduce friction**
- **Communicate to move people to action**
- **Adapt quickly to seize windows of opportunity**

Access your **FREE** bonus materials at
bonus.fasttrackyourbigidea.com

GLOSSARY

*The two most engaging powers of an author are
to make new things familiar and familiar things new.*
Samuel Johnson, poet, playwright, and biographer

My goal with this book is to present strategic business ideas in simple, straightforward language, avoiding jargon and keeping acronyms to a minimum.

But sometimes you might stumble upon a term that leaves you scratching your head. If you *do*, don't worry! You'll find a comprehensive glossary at bonus.fasttrackyourbigidea.com with definitions, frameworks, thought leaders and indexed references that point to where each term appears in the book.

Suggestions for additions are always welcome!

NOTES

1   Exodus 4:10-12 Holy Bible, New International Version®, NIV®
    Copyright ©1973, 1978, 1984, 2011 by Biblica, Inc.®

2   The Honorable Matthew S. Collier, "Unexpected Leadership,"
    Thayer, January 1, 2017, https://www.thayerleadership.com/
    blog/2017/unexpected-leadership.

3   Devon Delfino, "Percentage of Businesses That Fail—and How
    to Boost Chances of Success," LendingTree, last modified April
    8, 2024, https://www.lendingtree.com/business/small/fail-
    ure-rate/.

4   Dileep Rao, "Unlock Success: 8 Proven Strategies to Beat the
    ~80% VC-Venture Failure Rate," Forbes, September 28, 2023,
    https://www.forbes.com/sites/dileeprao/2023/09/28/unlock
    -success-8-proven-strategies-to-beat-the-80-vc-venture-failure
    -rate/.

5   Boris Ewenstein, Wesley Smith, and Ashvin Sologar, "Changing
    change management," McKinsey & Company, July 1, 2015,
    https://www.mckinsey.com/featured-insights/leadership/
    changing-change-management.

6   Team EMB, "Overcoming Challenges in Data Transformation
    Projects," Expand My Business, November 27, 2023, https://
    blog.emb.global/challenges-in-data-transformation-projects/.

7   Tracy Ebarb, "Nonprofits Fail—Heres Seven Reasons Why,"
    Inside Charity, accessed April 28, 2024, https://insidecharity.
    org/2019/09/07/nonprofits-fail-heres-seven-reasons-why-tracy
    -ebarb/.

8   World Uncertainty Index, accessed April 27, 2024, https://world
    uncertaintyindex.com/.

9   Dana Maor, Michael Park, and Brooke Weddle, "Raising the
    resilience of your organization," McKinsey & Company, October
    12, 2022, https://www.mckinsey.com/capabilities/people-and
    -organizational-performance/our-insights/raising-the-resilience
    -of-your-organization.

10 "LSA 3x Organizational Alignment Research," LSA Global,
    accessed April 27, 2024, https://lsaglobal.com/insights/
    proprietary-methodology/lsa-3x-organizational-alignment
    -model/.

11 "Everett M. Rogers's Research while affiliated with University of
    New Mexico and other places," ResearchGate, accessed April
    27, 2024, https://www.researchgate.net/scientific-contributions
    /Everett-M-Rogers-5273466.

12 Visual inspired by concepts from Everett M. Rogers, *Diffusion of Innovations*, 5th ed. (Simon and Schuster, 2003) and from Geoffrey Moore, *Crossing the Chasm: Marketing and Selling High-Tech Products to Mainstream Customers* (Harper Business Essentials, 1991).

13 Visual inspired by concepts from William Bridges and Susan Bridges, *Managing Transitions: Making the Most of Change* (Da Capo Lifelong Books, 2017).

14 Michele Wucker, *You Are What You Risk: The New Art and Science of Navigating an Uncertain World* (Pegasus Books, 2021).

15 "The Lloyd's Register Foundation World Risk Poll," Lloyd's Register Foundation, accessed April 27, 2024, https://wrp. lrfoundation.org.uk/. Refers to 2021 World Worry Index Survey data.

16 Thomas Stanton, TEDx Talks, "Enterprise Risk Management | Thomas H. Stanton | TEDxJHUDC," March 20, 2017, YouTube, video, 9:03, https://youtu.be/voGyHN-tWMg?si=GNhA1Wf27i0ItB53.

17 Simon Sinek, *Start with Why: How Great Leaders Inspire Everyone to Take Action* (Portfolio, 2009).

18 "Our Story," Bitty and Beau's Coffee, accessed April 28, 2024.

19 Visual inspired by The Business Model Canvas (BMC) by Alex Osterwalder and Yves Pigneur, available for use under a Creative Commons license from Strategized AG. https:// en.wikipedia.org/wiki/Business_Model_Canvas.

20 Angus Fletcher, *Storythinking: The New Science of Narrative Intelligence* (Columbia University Press, 2023).

21 Niharika Hariharan Joshi, Hamza Khan, and Istvan Rab, "A design-led approach to embracing an ecosystem strategy," McKinsey & Company, July 21, 2021, https://www.mckinsey. com/capabilities/mckinsey-design/our-insights/a-design-led -approach-to-embracing-an-ecosystem-strategy#/.

22 Image inspired by Lean and Six Sigma concepts, shared by the American Society for Quality, Quality Tools, Impact-Effort Matrix, accessed April 28, 2024, https://asq.org/quality -resources/impact-effort-matrix.

23 Solomon Asch, Article on Asch Conformity Experiments, accessed April 28, 2024, https://en.wikipedia.org/wiki/Asch _conformity_experiments.

24 Image inspired by Solomon Asch, "Conformity – Asch (1951)," Tutor2u, last modified September 6, 2022, https://www. tutor2u.net/psychology/reference/conformity-asch-1951.

25 Aaron De Smet, Tim Koller, and Dan Lovallo, "Bias Busters: Getting both sides of the story," McKinsey & Company, September 4, 2019, https://www.mckinsey.com/capabilities/strategy-and-corporate-finance/our-insights/bias-busters-getting-both-sides-of-the-story.

26 Chris Voss, *Never Split the Difference: Negotiating as if Your Life Depended on It* (Harper Business, 2016), chapter 5.

27 Image inspired from research about Mendelow's Matrix including "What Is Mendelow's Matrix And How Is It Useful?", Oxford College of Marketing, last modified 2024, https://blog.oxfordcollegeofmarketing.com/2018/04/23/what-is-mendelows-matrix-and-how-is-it-useful/.

28 Charles Osgood, condensed version republished by Organization Builders, accessed April 28, 2024, https://www.organizationbuilders.com/content1/responsibiltypoem.

29 Martin Reeves et al., "Signal Advantage," Boston Consulting Group, February 22, 2010, https://www.bcg.com/publications/2010/strategy-signal-advantage.

30 Jim Collins, *Good to Great: Why Some Companies Make the Leap . . . and Others Don't* (Harper Business, 2001).

31 Susan Scott, *Fierce Conversations: Achieving Success at Work and in Life One Conversation at a Time* (Berkley, 2004).

32 Brian Christian, *The Alignment Problem: Machine Learning and Human Values* (W. W. Norton & Company, 2020).

33 "For Employees, Shared Values Matter More Than Policy Positions," Qualtrics, last modified June 2, 2022, https://www.qualtrics.com/news/for-employees-shared-values-matter-more-than-policy-positions/.

34 Blue Beyond Consulting, "'The Great Resignation': A Majority of Employees Would Quit Their Job—and Only 1 in 4 Workers Would Accept One—If Company Values Do Not Align with Personal Values," PR Newswire, October 20, 2021, https://www.prnewswire.com/news-releases/the-great-resignation-a-majority-of-employees-would-quit-their-job--and-only-1-in-4-workers-would-accept-one--if-company-values-do-not-align-with-personal-values-301404919.html.

35 Trish Sammer, "What a 13th-Century Monk Can Teach Us about Managing Information Overload," *Ladders*, February 28, 2021, https://www.theladders.com/career-advice/what-a-13th-century-monk-can-teach-us-about-managing-information-overload.

36 Jim VandeHei, Mike Allen, and Roy Schwartz, *Smart Brevity: The Power of Saying More with Less* (Workman Publishing Company, 2022).

37 "Multitasking: Switching costs," American Psychological Association, March 20, 2006, https://www.apa.org/topics/research/multitasking.

38 Jordan Gaines Lewis, "This Is How the Brain Filters Out Unimportant Details," *Psychology Today*, February 11, 2015, https://www.psychologytoday.com/us/blog/brain-babble/201502/is-how-the-brain-filters-out-unimportant-details.

39 Veronica Combs, "8 hours and 27 minutes. That's how long the average gamer plays each week," TechRepublic, March 10, 2021, https://www.techrepublic.com/article/8-hours-and-27-minutes-thats-how-long-the-average-gamer-plays-each-week/.

40 Ben Decker and Kelly Decker, *Communicate to Influence: How to Inspire Your Audience to Action* (McGraw Hill, 2015).

41 Robert B. Zajonc, "Mere Exposure: A Gateway to the Subliminal," *Association for Psychological Science* 10, no. 6 (2001): 224-228, doi: 10.1111/1467-8721.00154.

42 Paul M. Leonardi, Tsedal B. Neeley, and Elizabeth M. Gerber, "How managers use multiple media: Discrepant events, power, and timing in redundant communication," *Organization Science* 23, no. 1 (2012): 98-117, doi: 10.1287/orsc.1110.0638.

43 Henry Blodgett, "LinkedIn's CEO Jeff Weiner Reveals the Importance of Body Language, Mistakes Made out of Fear, and One Time He Really Doubted Himself," *Business Insider*, September 22, 2014, https://www.businessinsider.com/linkedin-ceo-jeff-weiner-on-leadership-2014-9#ixzz3TaXO2Buy.

44 NASA, "Mars Climate Orbiter," Jet Propulsion Laboratory, accessed May 1, 2024, https://www.jpl.nasa.gov/missions/mars-climate-orbiter.

45 Alan Iny, Hans Kuipers, and Alison Sander, "Building Your Uncertainty Advantage," Boston Consulting Group, July 29, 2020, https://www.bcg.com/publications/2020/using-uncertainty-to-your-advantage.

46 Joerg Esser, "The Secret of Adaptable Organizations Is Trust," Harvard Business Review, March 15, 2021, https://hbr.org/2021/03/the-secret-of-adaptable-organizations-is-trust.

47 Goodwill Industries International, "Goodwill's Heritage, Mission, Vision, and Values," accessed January 14, 2025, https://www.goodwill.org/about-us/goodwills-heritage-mission-vision-and-values/.

48 James Clear, *Atomic Habits: An Easy and Proven Way to Build Good Habits and Break Bad Ones* (Avery, 2018).

49 Rollin McCraty and Doc Childre, "The Grateful Heart: The Psychophysiology of Appreciation," in The Psychology of Gratitude, ed. Robert A. Emmons and Michael E. McCullough (Oxford University Press, 2004), 230-256, https://doi.org/10.1093/acprof:oso/9780195150100.003.0012.

50 Erin Bryant, "Dopamine affects how brain decides whether a goal is worth the effort," National Institutes of Health, March 31, 2020, https://www.nih.gov/news-events/nih-research-matters/dopamine-affects-how-brain-decides-whether-goal-worth-effort.

51 Annlia Paganini-Hill, Claudia H. Kawas, and Maria M. Corrada, "Positive Mental Attitude Associated with Lower 35-Year Mortality: The Leisure World Cohort Study," *Journal of Aging Research* 2018 (2018), doi: 10.1155/2018/2126368.

52 Damien Smith, "How Williams Overcame Its Greatest F1 Setback," *Motorsport*, last modified November 29, 2021, https://www.motorsport.com/f1/news/how-williams-overcame-its-greatest-setback/4802933/.

53 Ronald A. Heifetz, Marty Linsky, and Alexander Grashow, *The Practice of Adaptive Leadership: Tools and Tactics for Changing Your Organization and the World* (Harvard Business Press, 2009).

IN APPRECIATION

Writing a book to help people fast track big ideas is a big idea. A community of amazing people helped me cross the finish line.

I am grateful to the hundreds of individuals and organizations who contributed to the principles and stories in this book. I appreciate the managers, colleagues, and clients who allowed me to experiment and learn these principles over the years. Whether I learned from afar or stumbled into potholes by your side, your pursuit of big ideas and tenacity to get back on track inspired me. Many of you took time to humbly share your learnings and scars. While I could not include every name and story, your fingerprints are all over this book. It has been an honor to learn with you.

Writing a book is a bigger adventure than it may seem. Thank you to the Mirasee community, especially to Lisa Bloom, Kristin Vesa and Jay Allyson, and to The Writer's Ally team. A special thanks to my sparring partners Nora Bellot and Steve Robbins, and to my artist and copyediting magicians, Nissa Milberger and Februalin Paquera Briones.

I am incredibly grateful to those who generously gave their time to provide feedback as I evolved this manuscript: Chantal Boeckman, Howard Fields, Robert Fukui, Wes Kimes, Kenjie Kirimi, Michelle Klein, Ana Maria Lowry, Deborah Malone, Tom Ruch, Darlene Schindel, Patrice Tsague, Taly Walsh, Allison Wilkerson, and Rebecca Yokomoto. Your challenging and constructive insights refined my points and sparked new ideas for serving others with this content.

To my adventure husband Bob, our children, and our parents, thank you for your unending encouragement. You never doubted I could do this!

Finally, I am grateful to God for wiring me with the energy and enthusiasm for big ideas and for giving me the courage to take risks for Him. With God, all things are possible.

●

ABOUT THE AUTHOR

Susan Schramm is on a mission to help people turn big ideas into reality. Whether in a boardroom, on a stage, in a classroom, or at a coffee shop, she finds joy in equipping and encouraging people to overcome obstacles and drive meaningful impact.

After decades of working with Fortune 500 companies, startups, and nonprofits to launch new products, programs, partnerships, and ventures, Susan founded Go to Market Impact, a business consultancy dedicated to helping leaders navigate the complexities of high-stakes strategies.

Susan created the DE-RISK SYSTEM FOR IMPACT® to help leaders proactively plan for the "people side of risk"—a critical yet often overlooked factor in strategic success. She brings energy, experience, and practical insights that inspire fresh perspectives and drive lasting results.

Insatiably curious about the world around her, Susan has proudly conquered one of her bucket-list goals: visiting all 50 states in the US. She is fueled by faith, family, and a bottomless cup of coffee.

Learn more about Susan at susanschramm.com or connect at www.linkedin.com/in/susanbaileyschramm.

www.ingramcontent.com/pod-product-compliance
Lightning Source LLC
Chambersburg PA
CBHW061020220326
41597CB00016BB/1760